THE
INDIA
WAY

Celebrating
30 Years of Publishing
in India

Select Praise for *The India Way*

'One of the many interesting aspects of *The India Way* is the use of a rare lens – the Mahabharata – to frame the current global strategic problems and India's foreign policy challenges. Jaishankar's judgments on themes ranging from non-alignment to balance of power will surely draw much critical interest within India and beyond. There is no doubt that the book opens an important window into Delhi's changing worldview ... The emerging cohort of strategic communities can and must learn from all traditions of statecraft – including Western, Chinese and Indian. The last few decades have unsurprisingly seen an explosion of international studies on the Chinese tradition of statecraft. Jaishankar's *The India Way* is a timely call to fill the deficit on the Indian end.'

– C. Raja Mohan, *Indian Express*

'Nothing should distract from the book's fundamental objective, namely, the elucidation of India's vision of itself and its behavior in global politics ... *The India Way* offers an utterly authentic vision of how the official mind in India imagines the country's international posture. To say that this volume is brilliant in both style and substance would be an understatement ... It should be indispensable reading.'

– Ashley J. Tellis, Carnegie Endowment for International Peace

'*The India Way* is a meditation on the sources of India's conduct on the global stage, and on the evolution of Indian foreign policy at a time of unprecedented changes in the global order. Dr Jaishankar's credentials are impeccable when it comes to dissecting India's options in an increasingly turbulent world. And he does so with a scholar's sincerity and a practitioner's panache.'

– Harsh V. Pant, *Hindustan Times*

'*The India Way* is a timely message to the new India which is becoming stronger and is seeking its due place in the world. The book is not a mere academic analysis or erudite exercise. It is the call of a serving External Affairs Minister with experience of four decades of distinguished career as a diplomat ... Jaishankar's bold, dispassionate, candid and clear articulation fits the description of diplomacy by Thiruvalluvar in his poem: "Diplomacy is articulation according to the need of the time with profound knowledge and without fear."'

– R. Viswanathan, *The Week*

'Rarely does an incumbent foreign minister have the time or inclination to write a book on foreign policy. But when a seasoned practitioner of diplomacy with a scholastic mind like Dr S. Jaishankar is in the saddle, a long work drawing upon deep reflection is not out of turn. *The India Way* is both an act of self-expression by a keen observer and lover of international relations, and a vehicle to communicate to the world how India is adapting to historic changes ... This book is educative about what the future holds for an aspirational country. It is a clarion call to play the game of realpolitik.'

– Sreeram Chaulia, *Asian Age*

'Some books are read for who has written them; some are for the contents, and some for style. One should read Dr S Jaishankar's book for all three. A former Foreign Secretary of India and now its Foreign Minister, Jaishankar has written on what could be a strategy for India, with an interesting style of weaving a story through looking back (from Awadh and even Mahabharata) to look ahead.'

– D. Suba Chandran, The Book Review Literary Trust

'S. Jaishankar lays out the broad framework of India's policymaking. He emphasizes a realistic approach free of dogmas, willing to take risks and ready to engage different powers at the same time. He offers an overview of the evolution of India's foreign policy through the pitfalls and the opportunities ahead ... The foreign policy framework *The India Way* offers is an authoritative account of New Delhi's worldview.'

– Stanly Johny, *The Hindu*

S. JAISHANKAR

THE INDIA WAY

STRATEGIES FOR AN UNCERTAIN WORLD

HarperCollins *Publishers* India

First published in hardback in India by
HarperCollins *Publishers* 2020

First published in paperback in India by
HarperCollins *Publishers* 2022
4th Floor, Tower A, Building No. 10, Phase II, DLF Cyber City,
Gurugram, Haryana – 122002
www.harpercollins.co.in

6 8 10 9 7

P-ISBN: 978-93-9440-721-3
E-ISBN: 978-93-9016-387-8

Typeset in 11/15 Berling LT Std
Manipal Technologies Limited, Manipal

Printed and bound at
Thomson Press (India) Ltd

For

K. Subrahmanyam, father

and

Aravinda R. Deo, mentor

Contents

Preface to the Paperback Edition
One Trend, Four Shocks

———

Events far away can have a dramatic impact on our daily lives and immediate surroundings. If any of us had doubts, the Covid pandemic has put those fully to rest. In a very different way, the consequences of the Ukraine conflict raised our awareness of the implications of globalization. Indifference to global developments is no longer affordable; in fact, it is downright dangerous. To most people, however, foreign policy by its very nature tends to be focused on the 'foreign' part. It immediately evokes distance and divergence. It suggests 'other' people who speak, think and act differently. All of that may be true but the growing reality is that foreign policy has now reached our homes.

It is something of an irony that well before the pandemic hit us, the world had come to terms with 'going viral'. The rapidity, seamlessness and interpenetration of our era were exhibited across domains. Economically, it was expressed as a centralized globalization that elevated 'just in time' to a religion. Politically, it spawned a borderless culture with an entitlement to intervene. Socially, it encouraged a global elite who could comfortably sit in judgment over the world. Diplomatically, it enabled gaming the system and weaponizing the normal. Technologically, we entered an existence of great promise and huge vulnerabilities. Never mind that each had a cost, until of course the aggregate risk made it hard to duck the difficult questions. The virus may be the key challenge in global health, but pervasiveness is now a reality in various aspects of our life. And each, in a sense, has a compulsion to return to checks and balances. Jobs, quality of life and privacy matter, just as do sovereignty, cultures and security. They cannot be left at the mercy of ostensibly anonymous global forces.

If that be the case, then it is imperative that we have a better sense of the world we live in. And, even more, of the changes that it is undergoing. Of course, the global order is always evolving, and in that sense, change could well be seen as a constant factor. But if we look at it relatively, the pace of transformation has definitely quickened. Especially after the 2008 global financial crisis, the comparative weight of major nation states has undergone a significant shift. New centres of production and consumption have come up with the accompanying political consequences. This drives the rebalancing of the order as we knew it earlier. That ongoing evolution has now been given a sharper edge due to the impact of the coronavirus pandemic, developments in Afghanistan, the Ukraine conflict and greater friction among key powers. 'One Trend and Four Shocks' are creating a new landscape. Appreciating their cumulative implications is not easy.

Prominent among their features is the revival of the case for strategic autonomy. This resurrection is taking place because of the stresses caused by disruptions, coercion and conflicts. The 'Four Shocks' have, each in their own way, created greater global anxiety and insecurity. In the last two years, we have seen supply chains disrupted and markets distorted by Covid. Concerns about reliability and resilience have been aggravated by worries of trust and transparency. The impact of the Ukraine conflict has been visible in sectors ranging from energy and metals to grain and fertilizers. Economic measures instituted in that context have broken radically new ground. Indeed, they have demonstrated how double-edged global linkages can become. The ideational facets of volatility have been as significant as the material ones. The Afghanistan outcome is profoundly consequential in this respect.

This is not just an India-centric debate on strategic autonomy, as in the past, but one more widespread, including even in Europe and the US. The concept itself has undergone a radical change due to globalization. Strategic autonomy can no longer be visualized as keeping a safe distance from dominant players. It is instead a derivative of capabilities, allowing the fending off of pressures and the exercise of choices. Nor should it be seen as autarky, a national state that is unsustainable in reality. On the contrary, more vigorous participation in the world economy due to higher performance gives a country many more cards in the games that nations play. For India, that is summed up by 'Atmanirbhar Bharat', 'Make in India' and 'Make for the World'.

Within this complex picture, there are some aspects that merit particular consideration. The Indo-Pacific, for example, is both a return of history and a manifestation of modernity. The significance of the Quad has been widely recognized, becoming the subject of considerable discussion. Finding and even keeping the right partners in a changing environment will obviously not be easy. India has its task cut out. The optimal solution would be to preserve the most advantageous from earlier experiences, without hesitating to explore new opportunities. The black-and-white analysis of the previous era, however, cannot be an accurate guide any longer. After all, we have now entered a world of convergences where the overlaps of interests are rarely perfect. With various nations, India will agree or not to differing degrees. This will be even more so as our influence broadens out. Thus, the defining geo-political and geo-economic issues of the day, including Indo-Pacific, Afghanistan, terrorism, climate change, pandemics, talent mobility or digital growth, will each produce a particular set of partnerships. Their weight and effectiveness will differentiate the more strategic ones from the others.

As a rising power, India will continuously rub against an international order, parts of which may not always be amenable to its rise. Indeed, Newton's third law of politics dictates that the process of emergence will get tougher with time. The challenge that we face is not just from competing powers, but also a phenomenon of freezing advantageous moments by those dominant in an era. Even seventy-five years later, we are still largely operating in a 1945 framework from which India was excluded. It is manifested in multiple ways across broad domains. India is particularly disadvantaged in this regard vis-à-vis China. Adjusting the global order to contemporary realities is, therefore, a larger mission from which there is no respite. How this is best done is the resulting debate. But freezing the moment is not only the strategy of others. It is often an assumption that nations have about themselves, the result of either entrenched habits or an impactful experience. Persisting with outdated beliefs and unrealistic calculations in a changing environment can be costly. It is, therefore, imperative to revisit first principles constantly on the key challenges of our times.

Fashioning an effective contemporary approach to China is particularly relevant in this context. There are issues that the world at large grapples with and there are some that are specific to India. The growth and influence of China have clearly exceeded expectations. What has imparted a greater urgency to policy-making is the added element of its behavioural pattern. India is faced with a complicated conundrum resulting from China steadily eroding longstanding agreements. At the end of the day, the state of the border will determine the state of the relationship. A significant shift in posture cannot be devoid of consequences.

Given the transformational impact of technology on our lives, it is also natural that it should have a deep impact on national security. In a globalized world, the flow of ideas and influences makes it difficult to limit security concerns to national borders. This is not to say that the orthodox challenges have gone away. A diverse and pluralistic society like India should never forget that its fault lines could be exploited by competitors. This danger will probably increase as we acquire greater salience. As India sets about putting its own house in better order, that too will elicit a pushback from those who have a vested interest in our vulnerabilities. In such a scenario, reimagining security is essential. It will not only make us better aware of the threats we really face but also encourage the emergence of newer solutions.

Security, of course, is best ensured through stronger comprehensive national power. And for that to progress, a polity like India must be obsessively committed to continuous reform. Resting on past laurels – real or exaggerated – is just another form of national complacency. We cannot continue to benchmark ourselves against our own past; it is simply not ambitious enough. The pandemic offers possibilities for decisive changes in many domains. Seizing them confidently will only demonstrate how deeply national reform is connected to national security. The truth must be recognized that foreign policy choices are not determined just by defence and security, but equally by industrial and technology capacities. Or limitations thereof. Cultural rebalancing too constitutes an important aspect of India's evolution. Its global connections going back to the colonial era are being tested against the arrival of a less elitist and more rooted democracy at home. How interests and attitudes strike a balance will be worth watching. 'New India' is getting stronger by the day and the world must come to terms with it.

Conceptualizing the world in more operational terms is a sign of seriousness. As we have seen on the home front, resistance to change has been our weakness for too long. Even worse, we can end up confusing sloganeering with strategy. Non-alignment, for example, was relevant in its day but has had much less meaning once the Cold War came to an end. A defence of our key interests in a unipolar era that has receded is now giving place to its advance in a multipolar setting. As rebalancing gathers steam, an appropriate expression of our intent has to emerge. However untidy, some form of multiple engagements is more reflective of reality today. So too is the need to capture convergences and partial overlaps of interests in order to create issue-based coalitions.

Large civilizational states naturally seek to expand their freedom of choice while going up the global order. But we need to think beyond that underlying approach now. We are gradually an influencer, no longer just the influenced. Our vision of regions in our immediate vicinity is already undergoing a change, expressed in the policies of Neighbourhood First and SAGAR (Security and Growth for All in the Region). We have also developed a clearer view of the extended neighbourhood to the east, west and north. These are actualized through the Act East policy towards ASEAN (Association of Southeast Asian Nations), the Think West approach to the Gulf and the Central Asia initiative. At the global level, the endeavour is to engage all the major centres of power to ensure India's optimal positioning. And the first steps towards a larger global visibility have also been taken, be it in Africa, the Caribbean or the Pacific Islands.

Foreign policy, however, is more than just a strategizing exercise to advance our national interest. Its merits are usually debated in a vocabulary of a narrow circle. Often, that is also the case with developing its argumentation. A discourse detached from the ground can end up defying common sense. Normalizing the practice of cross-border terrorism in the name of diplomacy is one illustration. Advocating a strategic partnership despite a significant territorial dispute is another. Pursuing a free trade agreement divorced from market logic is also a telling example. So too is a refusal to exploit obvious convergences simply because they conflict with inherited ideologies. In the final analysis, the credibility of any policy would depend on how it impacts the average citizen. And a judgment on its success would depend on its ability to pass a smell test. It cannot just sound clever; it must also feel right.

The parameters for such a test are not that complicated. To start with, the nation must be more secure. Building on that, its development should progress better using foreign partnerships. On global issues, its influence in determining solutions is expected to be stronger. In the international arena, its standing as a polity and the stature of its leadership should be higher. And not least, the routine challenges faced by the common person in dealing with the world must be better addressed. Every Indian out in the world must have the confidence that we have his or her back. By each measure, much has happened in the last eight years. Operation Ganga, in that sense, is more than an evacuation; it is equally a message.

The India Way is a practitioner's viewpoint that is consciously grounded. It is aimed at multiple audiences. Internationally, it is an articulation of an Indian thought process meant to provide clarity and enhance comfort. The world must know us better as India's influence increases. With those insights, the likelihood of partnerships will grow, just as the prospect of misunderstanding will mitigate. But this is meant too for those Indians outside the business of foreign policy. They must realize that whatever their level of attention to the world, global happenings will not leave them alone. 'One Trend and Four Shocks' are proof enough. Beyond that, they are stakeholders in decisions made in the policy domain that deal with their direct interests. To them, my message is that foreign policy matters to you, perhaps more than you think. Just as we enrich domestic politics through vigorous argumentation, diplomatic choices will also be sounder with greater democratization. So, let the debate continue and hopefully extend to a larger circle than before. I hope that the paperback edition of *The India Way* can help that happen.

S. Jaishankar
March 2022

Introduction

'Wisdom is to live in tune with the mode of the changing world'

— THIRUVALLUVAR

It was unsettling to discover after four decades as a professional diplomat that many of the assumptions on which we had operated were now being called into question. But it did not follow from there that our experiences were suddenly irrelevant. On the contrary, it seemed that those who could most objectively assess the last many decades were best placed to anticipate the coming times. Seeking truth from facts is, however, not easy. If the pressure of political correctness is one challenge, the weight of accumulated dogma is no less. An equally difficult reconciliation is that between an adequate awareness of the global context, and yet viewing it from a hard-headed national perspective. This has been a persistent dilemma since Independence and the era of nationalism has only sharpened it further. These are some issues of an endeavour that has occupied me for the last two years.

In many ways, it was natural to put pen to paper on the subjects around which my life has revolved. An unpublished PhD thesis and an in-house history of the Indo-US nuclear deal provided some confidence to do so. Thus, it came about that after my tenure as Foreign Secretary ended in 2018, this initiative began through a fellowship with the Institute of South Asian Studies, Singapore. If the project kept changing form and content thereafter, much of that reflected the rapid pace of events in the world we live in. At some stage, I put aside the temptation of bringing in any aspects of a memoir, believing that they are better written by those who are no longer operational. Instead, my effort was to develop an argumentation on contemporary politics through interactions in different forums, keeping them as analytical and dispassionate as possible.

Looking at the world over these four decades from key vantage points was truly helpful in arriving at a detached view of its risks and possibilities. A professional initiation in Moscow taught me valuable lessons in great power politics, some perhaps unintended. Four stints dealing with the United States created a lasting interest in a polity whose confidence and resilience are quite unique. A long stay in Japan was an education in the nuances of East Asia, as indeed in the unrealized potential of our ties. And a shorter one in Singapore brought out the importance of adjusting to global happenings. Postings in Prague and Budapest heightened sensitivity to the currents of history. An absorbing but difficult tour in Sri Lanka was an invaluable politico-military experience. But, if there was one great learning, that was in a China that I caught at an inflection point in 2009. As Ambassador there, subsequently in the US, and then as Foreign Secretary, I have had a ringside view of recent global changes. Above all, interacting with our own leadership over many years at different levels of hierarchy had a value that is difficult to put in words. From that, the big takeaways were the importance of defining strategic goals, recognizing optimal outcomes and appreciating the interplay of politics and policy.

This book was developed in the course of the last two years through a series of events. Lectures given at think tanks, conferences or business forums form its core. They remain relevant in large measure but have been updated where required. 'The Lessons of Awadh' is a fusion of comments on various such occasions. 'The Art of the Disruption' draws on addresses to the Oslo Energy Forum, the Raisina Dialogue, the Sir Bani Yas Forum and the Centre for Strategic and International Studies. 'Krishna's Choice' was articulated in its essence at the Sai Foundation, New Delhi. 'The Dogmas of Delhi' is an expanded version of the Fourth Ramnath Goenka Memorial Lecture. 'Of Mandarins and Masses' is a hybrid of talks at St Stephen's College, the Heritage Foundation, the University of Birmingham and the Atlantic Council. 'The Nimzo Indian Defence' is based on a lecture delivered in Singapore. 'A Delayed Destiny' combines discussions at the Delhi Policy Group, India Foundation and the India International Centre. 'The Pacific Indian' owes its articulation to three Indian Ocean Conferences organized by the India Foundation and one by the National Maritime Foundation. And 'After the Virus' builds on recent speeches starting with the Fifth Raisina Dialogue 2020, taking into account the impact of the pandemic.

To the organizations that provided a platform to formulate and express my thoughts, I am profoundly grateful. Audience responses were helpful in developing the argumentation. If propositions are sometimes deliberately sharpened, it is only with an intention to set minds at work. Global developments are clearly the overarching context for an exercise in which our national performance is assessed. The coronavirus epidemic is not only a reminder of this reality but also a harbinger of changes that the world will now experience. To appreciate its consequences, what we require at home is a dispassionate debate that rises above competitive politics.

I am in debt to all those who have contributed to the making of this volume, especially an irreverent family, long suffering friends and argumentative colleagues. A special word of thanks

INTRODUCTION

to Radhika, Guru, Rajesh and Ramesh without whom these views would have never found expression. My publishers, especially Krishan Chopra, have been very patient as the fate of the book was linked to the twists and turns in my own life. I hope that their forbearance is rewarded.

1

The Lessons of Awadh

The Dangers of Strategic Complacency

————

'The heaviest penalty for declining to rule is to be ruled by someone inferior'

– PLATO

A famous Satyajit Ray film some decades ago captured the Indian self-absorption that shapes its larger awareness of the world. It depicted two Indian nawabs engrossed in a chess game while the British East India Company steadily took over their wealthy kingdom of Awadh. Today, as another global power rises – that too in India's immediate proximity – this country cannot be oblivious once again to its consequences. Ideally, the emergence of China should serve as an inspiration to sharpen India's competitive instincts. But at the very least, it should stir a serious debate about the direction of world politics and its implications for us.

This is important because in parallel there are other momentous shifts underway. A larger rebalancing was already in evidence, now overlaid by greater regional volatility, higher risk-taking, stronger nationalism and a rejection of globalization. But the critical change is the recalibrated posture of an America that has long been the bedrock of the contemporary international system. Its response to China's rise may well determine the direction of contemporary politics. Because global happenings are not always factored fully into its internal dynamics, such developments have often passed India by. How they impact its thinking is also not always made clear in the absence of definitive political narratives. So as India rises in the world order, it should not only visualize its interests with great clarity but also communicate them effectively.

This is an effort to contribute to that endeavour, encouraging an honest conversation among Indians, without discouraging the world from eavesdropping.

International relations may be mostly about other nations, but neither unfamiliarity nor indifference lessen its consequences. So, rather than allow events to come upon us, these are better anticipated and analysed. That has not been our history, as demonstrated in the Panipat syndrome that saw invading forces enter the Indian heartland for decisive battles. This default option of playing defence reflects a mindset that does not comprehend external events well, leave alone appreciate their implications.

In contemporary times, Indian agnosticism about the outcome of the Second World War had major repercussions. In the next decade, India's handling of the Cold War led Pakistan, a smaller neighbour, to close the power differential for decades. The consequences of its illegal occupation of part of Jammu and Kashmir was as underestimated as the strength of its revanchist sentiments after 1971. Understanding of China has been inadequate, whether it was the significance of the 1949 revolution, later the intensity of its Communist nationalism or, finally, the enormity of its post-1978 rise. As India developed a greater familiarity with world politics, power equations were misjudged by political romanticism. Inevitable decisions, such as on nuclear weapons, were consequently delayed at great cost. The issue of pursuing earlier a United Nations Security Council seat is another example that has been debated widely.

Missed opportunities in economic development by turning our back on global progress are, of course, a story told before. While the 1971 Bangladesh War, the 1991 economic reform, the 1998 nuclear tests and the 2005 nuclear deal were exercises in strategic retrieval, it nevertheless told on our overall standing. It is only more recently that a stronger realpolitik has overcome a complacency based on entrenched dogma.

The rise of a potential superpower is naturally a disruptive occurrence for any global order. If we forget that, it is because the last time it happened, with the USSR, was in the midst of a World War that masked its emergence. Transitions between superpowers and their overlapping coexistence are difficult at best of times. The one between the UK and the US in the first half of the twentieth century is the exception, not the rule. But when societies are built on different principles, then it is very much harder to reconcile contestation with collaboration. Divergences may matter less when a nation's influence is relatively small, and its actions mainly affect its own people. It was perhaps more acceptable in the immediate post-colonial world, when capabilities were of a lesser order. But once they reach a global scale, it became much harder to overlook. Conducting international relations, while being agnostic about the character of societies, has its limitations. This is strikingly evident today as attitudes across the political divide reinforce each other. Even as this started happening, globalization as a powerful compulsion for cohabitation initially mitigated emerging contradictions. At some stage, however, geopolitical stresses have found articulation as a vocal nationalism among states that feed off each other. Sharper competitiveness should be expected as the driving force of the world today.

China's full-blown arrival on the global stage has inevitably had its repercussions. Some of that arises from the natural displacement of other powers. But part of it is also because of China's unique characteristics. Unlike other nations that rose earlier in Asia, it is much harder to fit into the Western-led global order. The reality now is that the two most powerful nations of our day who served each other's purpose politically for many years now no longer do so.

For India, such a scenario raises a host of strategic challenges. Handling that adroitly will be important, especially when approaching it from the perspective of our own interests. Developing the mindset to not only respond but actually leverage that is what could define the new India. The US currently is back to the strategic drawing board as it reinvents itself. Its interim approach is of greater individualism, more insularity and sharp retrenchment. This exercise of recalculation is a difficult one because the consequences of its past strategic bets cannot be easily undone. So we hear a potent narrative of unfair trade, excessive immigration and ungrateful allies. And market access, technology strengths, military dominance and the power of the dollar now seem to be the ingredients of an emerging solution. Whatever the politics that unfolds in America, much of the change is there to stay. The US-China dynamic that will impinge on the two States themselves and on the world is the global backdrop for Indian policymaking.

The era of benign globalization that facilitated the dramatic rise of China has come to an end. How this came to pass is obviously important; what to make of it even more so. India's rise has been slower and will now have to navigate difficult waters. We have entered a turbulent phase where a new kind of politics is being fashioned. The issue is not whether India will continue rising; that vector is reasonably assured. The question is how to do so optimally in an era of greater uncertainty.

For the near term, India has little choice but to pursue a mix of multiple approaches, some orthodox and others more imaginative. But in all of them, partnerships with global interests could make a significant difference. Much of that would revolve around the West and Russia. But China, now the world's second largest economy, can hardly be disregarded in any calculation.

Leveraging them all may not be easy but still no less necessary for that. Mastering mind games and playing hardball are also musts in a more visceral world. To do all that, it is vital that we come to terms with its complex dynamics. Only then can India successfully execute strategic policies for a new era.

Events in the last few years have been such a deviation from the norm that there is understandable confusion about the direction of world affairs. Both in the case of the US and China, developments have been outside the realm of earlier experiences. Pakistan has exceeded the most pessimistic projection of its policies. Other neighbours of India have sometimes acted at odds with their past. The influence of changing geopolitics is visible in our immediate vicinity, as in the extended neighbourhood. Refreshing India's ties with Russia has required dedicated efforts. Japan has offered opportunities notwithstanding the complexity of its predicament. Comfort with Europe has grown, but needs more insights into its increasingly intricate politics. Much of our analyses of current happenings are also coloured by ideological battles. Whether we like the direction of events or not, it does not make them less real. They have both causes and effects that must be acknowledged. Whatever our views, it is better to analyse than just demonize the phenomenon that is Donald Trump.

When the dominant power in the world revisits first principles, its consequences are profound. Assessing that accurately is part of gauging the permanence of the change underway. For India, the exercise holds particular importance because American calculations have been supportive of its recent rise. How much a shift in its thinking would transform world politics and affect India's interests is today a paramount question. It is inextricably linked to the dynamics of its relationship with other powers. The new American approach to trade and security is no less relevant. It would be a mistake to approach the Trump Administration using the logic of previous experience with predecessors. There are new priorities in the making and the old playbook of dealing with that country needs rewriting.

India's rise will inevitably be compared to that of China, if only because that country has immediately preceded it. Its imprint on global consciousness, its civilizational contribution, geopolitical value and economic performance will all be factors in that exercise. Emulating the strategies and diplomatic tactics of another obviously cannot be a serious proposition for a society with a very different history and outlook. That said, there is much that India can learn from China. One important lesson is demonstrating global relevance as the surest way of earning the world's respect. The Singaporean leader Lee Kuan Yew once paid India's rise a back-handed compliment of being the more reassuring one. Today's world may call for a greater willingness to make waves.

There could also be an opportunity in a world looking for more sources of growth and stability. Being a democratic polity, a pluralistic society and a market economy, India will grow with others, not separately. Given these affinities, such an India can exploit effectively a search for new partnerships. Values that bring them together do matter, probably even more so in a technology-driven world. They shape intent that when paired with capabilities determines the nature of power. If one is less suspect, then there would be greater enthusiasm in welcoming the other.

Geopolitics and balance of power are the underpinning of international relations. India itself has a tradition of Kautilyan politics that put a premium on them. If there are lessons from the near past, it is that these were not given the weightage that they deserved. The Bandung era of Afro-Asian solidarity in the 1950s serves as a reminder of the costs of neglecting hard power. But more than lack of focus on capabilities, they reflect an underlying thinking. We have since reached a league where the ability to protect our interests is an assumption, not just an option. That is best done through a mix of national strengths and external relationships.

Clearly, in a more nationalistic world, diplomacy will use competition to extract as much gains from as many ties as possible. But there is, nevertheless, a strong case for India also supporting a greater sense of order. Our own growth model and political outlook intrinsically favour rules-based behaviour. India must make a virtue of reconciling global good with national interest. The challenge is to practise that successfully in a world of greater multipolarity and weaker multilateralism.

India's foreign policy carries three major burdens from its past. One is the 1947 Partition, which reduced the nation both demographically and politically. An unintended consequence was to give China more strategic space in Asia. Another is the delayed economic reforms that were undertaken a decade and a half after those of China. And far more ambivalently. The fifteen-year gap in capabilities continues to put India at a great disadvantage. The third is the prolonged exercise of the nuclear option. As a result, India has had to struggle mightily to gain influence in a domain that could have come so much more easily earlier. It is, of course, better that these issues are being addressed late than never. But greater self-reflection on our mistakes since 1947 would certainly serve the nation well. We could also extend that to the roads not taken.

For a country that has long operated in a disadvantageous landscape, any change is to be welcomed with an open mind. While more distant developments cannot be disregarded, those in our immediate vicinity offer even greater promise. A Neighbourhood First approach that generously rebuilds economic and societal linkages of the Subcontinent can work to India's favour. Extending the sense of neighbourhood to the East and the West is almost as important. Integrating the sea space to the South into our security calculus is the other key element of a broader vision. Together, the successful execution of such policies can reverse much of the strategic implications of the downsizing of India.

The endeavours of the ASEAN to retain its cohesion and centrality also creates a demand for India. If the Asian balance of power was skewed by the Partition, this was further aggravated by the post-1945 restraints on Japan. The security posture of that polity therefore has some implications for India's calculations. In fact, when it comes to Asia, the extent of change is still far from fully apparent. What can be safely asserted is that the openings for India are more, not less.

However unsettling the current world picture may look, it should not mask the progress made in the last few decades. In a vast range of domains, they have transformed the quality of life for many. Certainly, Indians would be justified in expecting the future to be better. They cannot ignore global disruptions, but have no reason to buy into a pessimistic outlook. On the contrary, our domestic situation and international positioning opens up many possibilities. The options we create will help determine the choices we make.

This is a time for us to engage America, manage China, cultivate Europe, reassure Russia, bring Japan into play, draw neighbours in, extend the neighbourhood and expand traditional constituencies of support. The mix of opportunities and risks presented by a more uncertain and volatile world is not easy to evaluate. Structural changes are even harder to come to terms with, especially the diminution of regimes and disregard of rules. Goals, strategy and tactics are all today very different. The deficit in global goods may be troubling, but there are no ready substitutes.

In such a dynamic situation, creating a stable balance in Asia is India's foremost priority. It is only a multipolar Asia that can lead to a multipolar world. Equally important, it would put a premium on India's value for the global system. Our approach should be to build comfort with the world, not opaqueness or distance. There will be a natural suspicion of all rising powers that we will have to allay. Taking on global responsibilities, acting as a constructive player and projecting our own distinct personality are elements of that solution. India is better off being liked than just being respected.

So what will this really mean in terms of foreign policy and its practices? To begin with, it would require advancing national interests by identifying and exploiting opportunities created by global contradictions. Such an India would pay more attention to national security and national integrity. It would not be hesitant in adjusting its positions where required by its own interests. This mindset would also accord primacy to the nurturing of goodwill, beginning with India's immediate neighbourhood. That would include a stronger sense of its bottom lines and a willingness to do what it takes to defend them. Making a visible impact on global consciousness would be taking this to the next level. It would encourage a greater contribution to global issues and regional challenges. Humanitarian assistance and disaster response (HADR) is an obvious platform to demonstrate a more forthcoming posture.

There would be conceptual aspects as well. Introducing our own diplomatic terms into the discourse is intrinsic to the process of international emergence. The Indo-Pacific, the Quad or the BRICS earlier are illustrative examples. Brand building that already plays on our IT and business strengths could be expanded further. The corona pandemic has allowed India to be now projected as the pharmacy of the world. Cultural practices can also be 'mainstreamed' to strengthen that process. Observing the International Day of Yoga or advocating traditional medicines are cases in point. Even the more prolific use of our own languages in interacting with the world is an indicator of the changing equilibrium.

But more than the promotional elements, it is the underlying assumptions that can make a difference. We have been conditioned to think of the post-1945 world as the norm and departures from it as deviations. In fact, our own pluralistic and complex history underlines that the natural state of the world is multipolarity. It also brings out the constraints in the application of power. A behaviour and a thought process which reflects that can facilitate the creation of a more favourable equilibrium with others.

Indian policymakers may need to assess the merits of more realism in their approach to world affairs. To a great extent, this is a compulsion forced on them by global developments. Increasing nationalism across geographies is contributing to a more transactional view of international relations. The primacy being given to trade and connectivity to shape choices strengthens these trends. An unabashed America First and a muscular China Dream are setting the tone. In any case, Russia's focus has long been narrower than that of the Soviet Union. But even a Europe with a growing fortress mentality is struggling to find the right balance between its interests and values. As for Japan, its continued caution speaks for itself. India has little choice but to do in Rome as Romans do. Indeed, it can do that really well and perhaps even find new opportunities in the process.

However, there is also a reason for brand differentiation that is especially important for a rising and aspirational power. In India's case, this should build on the positive aspects of its nationalism. The world must be reminded that we provided economic assistance and training to others even when our resources were meagre. The expansion of India's engagement with the world should be seen as something deeper than just ambition. The approach of '*Sabka Saath, Sabka Vikas, Sabka Vishwas*' is as relevant to foreign policy as to the domestic one. It should articulate a fundamental desire to engage the world more comprehensively.

What India and the world mean to each other will change as they develop new equations. An economy that is transitioning to a higher level will hold a different relevance. That will mean striking the right balance between developing stronger national capabilities, making it easier to do business, ensuring a level playing field, and growing with the global economy. New equilibriums between the world and India will arise in different fields, some of them not without friction. But the international community has much more riding on India than just economic gains. Its performance will determine whether Sustainable Development Goals targets are achieved, climate change challenges are addressed, disruptive technologies are adopted, global growth is balanced and accelerated, and a larger pool of talent is made available.

Not just that, it is also very much on India's record that the global credibility of democratic practices will be strengthened. For that, India must successfully take forward its own model in the years ahead. While the progress of what will be among the larger economies in the next generation will be carefully monitored, its relevance to the priorities of the world will attract even more attention. Central to that exercise will be the ability to deliver a credible Make in India programme that can contribute to more resilient global supply chains. No less significant will be the deployment of emerging and greener technologies on a scale that make for a global difference.

The socio-cultural changes that this India is undergoing are also an important factor in the overall matrix. Younger demographics and a broader awareness are contributing to stronger self-belief. An aspirational India will inevitably attach greater priority to pursuing national goals and establishing a global presence. Its greater sense of assurance will take India's explorations in many directions. It is necessary that contemporary international affairs recognize and respect that development.

As an Indian diplomat, I have watched the world change beyond imagination in the course of a long career. My generation and those before carried into our profession the heavy baggage of difficult experiences with the US, China and Pakistan. By the 1970s, these three accounts had mutated into a joint threat to Indian interests. The first half of my diplomatic life was dominated by two geopolitical realities: the Cold War and the rise of political Islam. They combined to precipitate the break-up of the Soviet Union, an event of great consequence for India. The second half saw our country come to terms with these changes and more. It fundamentally reshaped our ties with the US, even as a new power rose in the East with global repercussions. But it is not just the world that is changing; so too are Indian capabilities, aspirations and priorities.

All of this is cumulatively reflected in an evolution from the centrality of the Soviet relationship to convergences with multiple powers. Economic reform, the nuclear tests, the 2005 nuclear deal and a tougher national security posture are among its diplomatic milestones. Together, they helped create a policy outlook that has not been easy to capture in terms of orthodox thinking. If India drove the revived Quad arrangement, it also took membership of the Shanghai Cooperation Organization. A longstanding trilateral with Russia and China coexists now with one involving the US and Japan. These apparently contradictory developments only illustrate the world in which we now operate. Comprehending and messaging them is hard, especially to those not ready to come to terms with the intricacies of the new architecture. Positioning is of increasing value in a fluid world, explaining the importance of engaging competing powers like the US, China, the EU or Russia at the same time.

But when Indian actions are viewed from the perspective of its own self-interest, a clearer pattern starts to emerge. It is one of constant advancement of goals and interests, using all pathways that the world has to offer. And since that often means plunging into the unknown, it requires both judgement and courage. Our past will always be an influence, but no longer a determinant of our future. Forging ahead will mean taking risks and refraining from passing off timidity as strategy or indecision as wisdom.

In many ways, India's progress of the last five years has confounded those who have been unable or unwilling to transcend the old framework of analysis. Expectations that its America policy would founder initially on the ideology of one Administration or then on the nationalism of another were proved wrong. That India could stand firm on key concerns and yet establish a stable relationship with China was not easily appreciated. The structural basis for ties with Russia is underestimated, as also the relevance of Europe and Japan to contemporary India.

Perhaps the strongest preconceptions were in regard to the immediate neighbourhood. Every complication was depicted as a setback. And every correction was explained as an inevitable happening, presumably independent of India's action. That being the case, it is hardly a surprise that the transformed landscape in our vicinity was not even recognized.

Pakistan predictably has been the cause of the greatest debate. That India could offer a hand of friendship, but nevertheless respond strongly to acts of terror, is hardly a contradiction, except for those determined to see one. Clearly, different actions, players and times call for different responses. And setting the agenda to reflect contemporary challenges like terrorism is common sense, not wilfulness.

Those with a historical sense of our national security threats will understandably worry about Afghanistan. Whether we blame it on imperial overstretch or just plain misjudgement, matters there have come to a difficult pass. But it is also true that the clock cannot be turned back two decades. India has a hand to play because of its contributions during this time. And it has consequently a standing of its own that is of no small value. Therefore, it is important not to be stampeded by the tactical manoeuvres of others. We will count, not because of the largesse of the world, but due to our strengths. And our role will not just reflect that, but also our convergences with other interested powers.

Experience of governance always adds greater reality to any analysis. Simply put, many things are easy to advocate, much harder to do. In fact, this was precisely that argument with which my father tempted a student of international relations to sit for the Foreign Service examination in 1976. The learning since is that actual policy in a large country is a parallel pursuit of multiple priorities, some of whom could be contradictory. Neither abstention nor hedging are always answers to their pulls and pressures. Choices have to be made, not just debated. And they cannot be without costs.

But before choices comes the issue of capabilities. It is our ability to rise to domestic challenges that will determine India's place in the world. We are at least focused on the right issues now: digitization, industrialization, urbanization, rural growth, infrastructure, skills etc. The achievement of Sustainable Development Goals can be for India what the Millennium Development Goals did for China.

There will be decisions on the economic front that will have a direct bearing on our comprehensive national power. We have a record of both over-protecting and under-protecting different sectors. The post-1991 strategy has clearly gone astray and both the current trade wars and post-corona recovery are powerful compulsions to formulate a more contemporary approach. Similar to how it approaches political multipolarity, India will have to undertake its economic variant, especially the big hubs around which its trade and investments revolve. Technology too has a special resonance for a society given to leapfrogging. Aggressive deployment may be tough but offers great rewards. Eventually, leading abroad will require delivering at home.

Going up in the global power hierarchy, whether in terms of capability or influence, is only one element of India's rise. Our nation has other journeys to make in parallel. In the last few decades, we have heard more authentic voices as democratization took deeper roots. These changes in our national culture have been affirmed, amongst others, through political and electoral outcomes. At the same time, India is also transitioning from a civilizational society to a nation state. It involves assuming attributes that introduce discipline and formalism in aspects of our daily life. There are also problems left over from history – especially the Partition – that require fresh thinking. So, quite apart from its growing prominence, the world is today required to come to terms with this changing India.

The key questions pertaining to us reflect the global rebalancing underway. Will the world continue to define India, or will India now define itself? Awadh remains the symbol of the former to this day. But if it is now to be the latter, then it means not just new equilibriums with other powers but with the world order itself. India is today on a voyage of self-discovery and the lessons of Awadh are its surest compass in that quest.

2

The Art of the Disruption

The United States in a Flatter World

———

'*Sometimes by losing a battle, you find a new way to win a war.*'

— DONALD TRUMP

If you had believed the best minds of our times, this was not supposed to happen. But for two decades, China had been winning without fighting, while the US was fighting without winning. We speak here not just about outcomes in specific theatres or regions. It was even more about economic growth, political influence, and quality of life. As a result, along the way, America lost its famous optimism. Something had to give and it did, in the 2016 American presidential election. This obviously was not the only reason for that result. But through that one electoral event, the upholder of the international system turned revolutionary. And China, the rising power, finds itself defending the status quo – or at least the elements to its advantage.

The world faces an extraordinary prospect of its two leading players doing what it takes to win, and then some more. Their behavioural impact on each other and the world is now visible. In other circumstances, the US could be practising the art of the deal. But in an unfavourable landscape, it seems more focused on changing the terms of engagement. The need of the day apparently is to discard what no longer works for it. Deals may or may not follow. In the ultimate analysis, the ability of major powers to reach accommodation will shape our times. When 'black swans' meet 'grey rhinos', the very nature of the habitat undergoes transformation.

To the immediate beholder, these developments appear alarming. Especially so, if we focus on the events to the exclusion of trends. But international relations is an exercise of both forging convergences and managing divergences. Such dynamic processes will keep evolving while coexisting. At the extremes, they produce allies or create conflicts. But in an inter-dependent world, most relationships tend to settle down in the middle. Convergences even among competing powers is not unknown. The briefer examples include that of Germany and USSR after the First World War or the US and the USSR during the second one. In contrast, the trans-Atlantic bond between the UK and the US proved exceptionally durable. Somewhere in-between would be the UK-Japan partnership after the Meji Restoration that lasted half a century. China's collaboration with the USSR/Russia in the 1950s and again today is also noteworthy.

The US-China relationship that currently holds global attention has gone on for four decades, not a short span in modern times. Who benefited more in this period is a question to which we may get a different answer today than two decades ago. But because it was long enough to be taken as a given by two generations, we attribute to it a sense of being natural. We ask why it is under stress now, when we could wonder equally easily why it lasted that long. But beyond these two questions, what the world is arguing over is the continuing relevance of a system that the established powers devised but which was used so brilliantly by the rising one to advance its prospects.

Typically, convergences dilute as the parties concerned move towards closer parity. Or believe they do. That is true with the US and China today as it was with the US and USSR in 1948, or the UK and Japan in 1922. The absence of a shared adversary who drove the coming together also changes the situation. The defeat of Germany and Japan removed the compulsions for the continuance of the US-USSR partnership. The lower salience of Russia has been a factor for the changes in the US-China one. And not least, as the UK-US special relationship suggests, while social similarities can be an extraordinary binding force, dissimilarities can be equally divisive. It is tempting to see current events as an outcome of choices, dissimulation or even of egos. All of that may be true, but there is also the unending process of international relations at work.

The events of 2016 were more than exceptional in their nature. That the most powerful nation of our times should change course so sharply has a significance that is hard to overstate. While recognizing that, it should also be noted that these developments are not an entirely novel phenomenon. America First itself has a history, whose more controversial elements are sometimes evoked to criticize it. And its prioritizing of national interests at the cost of international responsibilities is something that spans the ideological divide. One might well ask what a Bernie Sanders foreign policy would have looked like. But in its earlier version, it was not yet an America of global magnitude and that is the real difference.

Russia too followed such an approach immediately after the break-up of the USSR in 1992. To varying degrees, other nations big and small practise it, even if they do not admit doing so. All of this is only explainable by the reaction of key political demographics to their economic predicament that they linked to developments in the world. Simply put, global supply chains were perceived as an economic threat, and immigration and mobility as a cultural one.

For many in Asia, it is difficult to comprehend the insecurities that globalization has created in the West. They have led to the left-right combination that helps the electoral success of nationalist candidates. Because the benefits of a more seamless global economy overshadowed the uneven distribution within societies and between them, there is today as much bewilderment at the turn of events as there is anger.

When the deep state joins the loud state in the US, a structural shift is well underway. What began as an unexpected political phenomenon has mainstreamed to some extent over the last three years. Even before the corona crisis, the influence of global supply chains and domination of technologies had given a sharp edge to growing trade frictions. The high stakes of this competition are underlined by the fact that it is in many ways about disruption itself. The resulting capabilities and their deployment could without exaggeration determine the future direction of the world. Part of the contest revolves around the utilization of big data. Equally consequential is control over key emerging technologies. The new contestation is about artificial intelligence and advanced computing, quantum information and sensing, additive robotics and brain-computer interface, advanced materials, hypersonics and biotechnology. Whoever harnesses disruptive technologies better will influence the world more. Major powers recognize this increasingly starkly. As trade disputes now assume much deeper connotations, the US, in particular, may end up contemplating a radically different industrial policy to suit its national security needs.

When new balances emerged, so did theories of the entrenched power resisting the rising ones. The Sparta-Athens example was cited, as indeed the UK-Germany conflict. But that is only one aspect of a phenomenon more complex than a clash foretold. For there is also evidence of the dominant helping the rise of the aspiring. China itself is a beneficiary, first of the assistance of the USSR in the 1950s, and then of the US since the 1970s. The truth is that these frictions are not fully structural nor always preordained. Every kind of example can be found in history.

Dissimilar powers such as the US, European ones or Japan have both made common cause and gone to war. Related ones within Europe too have done the same. Culture has a role, as do interests and circumstances. But in the final analysis, it is all about calculations and aspirations. Both are derivatives of leadership choices and societal sentiments; nothing is really inevitable. And because it boils down to human factors, values and beliefs do play their part in shaping world affairs.

Many of the discomforts today arise from differences on key issues like the relationship between the state, politics, society, business, faith and the markets. It is expressed in matters of personal freedoms and institutional firewalls. Sociology matters, especially once it assumes global proportions. This is at the heart of the predicament the world faces today. And creating common ground is, therefore, the hardest diplomatic challenge. Whether these contradictions could have been finessed a little longer is debatable. But political outcomes in key nations have made the question irrelevant anyway. The Sino-US competition in its new avatar will be a long and hard contest without clear outcomes. The likely scenario is of a twilight zone, where shifts in geopolitics are compounded by leaps of technology. The rise of a new global power was never going to be easy, and an order waiting to happen will look like chaos till it does.

In an inter-dependent and constrained world, it can only unfold through tensions and negotiations, adjustments and transactions. In this process, much will depend on what is allowed to take root. An America that consciously chooses to be a higher cost but more insular economy, a nationalistic but innovative technology creator, and a self-sufficient but more powerful military, will mean a very different ball game. There will always be voices that would urge an accommodation. Perhaps even a return to the past. There is a third choice as well, one that retains the national security outlook of the present, but which appreciates the value of alliances. So, how much the culture of disruption will lead to the art of the deal still remains to be seen.

What can India do to advance its goals in this disrupted world? Much of that would depend on its handling of the two principal actors – the US and China. This is not the first occasion when India faces such a predicament. We went through the Cold War, maintaining our independence in policymaking amidst all its complexities. Far from being a linear exercise, India made the adjustments required on stressful occasions. After the Chinese attack in 1962, it turned to the US to the extent of asking for air cover. In 1971, presented with the prospect of a US-China-Pakistan axis and a looming Bangladesh crisis, it concluded a virtual alliance with the USSR. Whenever crises receded, India went back to the middle path. As Russia weakened and China rose, a new binary prospect appeared in the making. There was a natural tendency to transpose the earlier syndrome on this emerging one. But the era after the Indo-US nuclear deal of 2005 showed how excessive caution lost the chance to make more than incremental gains.

For the fact is that a return to the past only accentuates our limitations and undermines confidence. It encourages risk aversion and prevents exploitation of new opportunities. At this stage of its rise, it is vital that India make the most of convergences with others. These may vary by the region or the issue. Where intersections of interest are multiple, it is perhaps best to just distrust and verify. Because global fluidity is so pervasive, India must address this challenge of forging more contemporary ties on every major account. Achieving an overall equilibrium will depend on how it fares on the individual ones.

In a world of more naked self-interest, nations will do what they have to do with less pretence. Hence, India must brace itself for what may be expected to come. It has to prepare for assertions of influence that will exploit power differentials, economic advantages and dependency of connectivity. And it can best respond with a logic that is understandable to the other party. We can, however, reasonably expect that even those more powerful have limited interest in an aggravation of ties. After all, they too operate in a world of multiple poles and greater choices. The future is, therefore, more one of management of differences and finding some stability in a changing dynamic. This will not be without problems and the key is to develop and sharpen strategic clarity. Even with neighbours with whom there are serious issues, there should be hope that the price of a pragmatic settlement will be less than the costs of a difficult relationship.

At the same time, the temptation to pursue illusory gains based on past constructs should be resisted. No serious practitioner of politics will accept that foregoing opportunities to leverage will ever be rewarded. India cannot give any other nation a veto on its policy options. This is particularly so in a world when all significant players are trying to be as open-ended on their own choices. Nor is there a basis to suggest that a modest Indian global profile will somehow be rewarded by polities who are intrinsically enamoured of strength. On the contrary, it is when options are available to be exercised – and from time to time actually are – that realism prevails. This applies to all countries, as even partners will always strive to better terms of transaction.

The tumultuous times we now live in are a far cry from the soothing mantras of globalization that we heard just a few years ago. Polarization permeates our world, whether in domestic politics or in inter-state relations. What the US and China are doing to each other is difficult enough. But what their behaviour will do to the rest of the world is even more impactful. It will change our thinking and in time create new habits and attitudes. Those will not be easily reversed, if ever. Some of us may imitate them; others may have no choice but to simply chafe. But all will react, one way or the other. When the smoke clears, a different global architecture will start to take form.

New equations and interests would have come into being. Single-minded pursuit of national interest will make our world look like a bazaar, with more players, less rules and greater volatility. As a result, goals are more immediate and approaches more tactical. Structures have weakened as interest in finding common ground recedes. New York, Geneva and Brussels are now symbols to run against. Advantages are asserted in a more transactional ethos with negotiators learning that to their cost. Erosion in trust has been sharp, especially for nations that are part of alliance systems. Dependability is now a growing question mark and friends and allies are no longer immune to pressures. In fact, everybody is fair game when big affinities no longer overlook smaller differences. As nationalism sharpens across regions, so does the characterization of diverging interests. Black and white are redefined even as 'Green on Blue' attacks enter the political domain.

But the fact is that there are stabilizing forces at work too, many from the earlier era. The caution of markets and the unpredictability of conflicts are constraining factors on extreme competition. Economic inter-dependence also limits the extent of political risk-taking. They will continuously contest the changes underway, generating heated arguments at home and abroad. So, even as nations play more roughly for narrower objectives, there would also be those who are prepared to settle for less. In the liberal world, this could mean limiting aspirations to pluralism, or just the defence of openness. When it comes to relationships and expectations, both believers and sceptics may converge where outcomes are uncertain. Given all these pulls and pressures, clarity and objectivity are the two attributes that will remain in short supply.

The trend till recently was firmly in the opposite direction. The world was not only more interlinked in its activities, but also confident in that thinking. We all spoke of a global village and saw globalization realized in a variety of practical ways. Technology was the great promise that we could see made us more connected with each passing day. The default solution to any significant challenge – whether promoting trade, addressing climate change or responding to terrorism – was through shared endeavours. However, all that has started to change. It is not that the 'me' did not exist before. But national and global interests were usually reconciled through a network of agreements, mechanisms and practices. Between nation states and the international community stood intermediaries, alliances, regional structures or like-minded partners. But this world, evolving steadily since 1945, stands eroded by disenchantment with globalization and anger at mercantilism. Its three key principles that we had taken for granted – access to global markets, value of global supply chains and reliance on global talent mobility – are all under stress. Players are moreover multiplying even as rules are weakening. The old order is visibly changing but the new one is not yet in sight.

While equations between nations may be disturbed, the churning within societies is no less relevant. If the world is not what it used to be, it is because the shelf life of old normals has expired. The story in the Western world is of sharp income inequality, pressures on jobs, stagnant quality of life and blame on 'outsiders'. Growing resentment that was left untended was finally given voice by black swan events. Brexit was the warning bell and Trump's election the real thing. Whether it was targeting plumbers from Poland, caricaturing immigrants from Mexico or castigating refugees from Africa, politics mobilized around cultural threats and economic grievances. Doing so, it revealed that the thinking of established elites had become outdated. Small wonder that their foreign policy outlook should also be questioned, be it advocacy of collective interests or arguments of common good.

Once departures from the norm were set in motion, justifications were not difficult to find. The unfairness of globalization emerged as a lightning rod, especially the parts that could be directed at others. Big Tech underwent a rapid transformation from being the great hope to the new threat. The emergence of new agendas obviously tested old players, whose confidence that power would socialize proved misplaced. Across the world, it is being given form by political nationalism that challenges the status quo. The developing world, especially Asia, may present a contrasting picture with stronger growth rates and higher aspirations. But it is still in the middle of rebalancing and its declaration of success are very premature. Because globalization served much of Asia well, we wrongly assumed that its optimism was shared universally. When global convergence weakens, its advocates everywhere find their positions undermined.

As alliances erode and the US steps back from major international commitments, the resulting anxiety may be wider than we think. Once globalization comes under attack, all its facets are subject to pressures. Opposition to globalized business will naturally undermine its governing rules and criticize the institutions that oversee it. Such a world view will also resent those commitments that do not serve its immediate goals.

It is no accident that the political counter to globalization should focus on immigration and job security. These are issues that resonate most effectively with Western electorates, despite their economic logic being questionable. But the foreigner is a convenient whipping boy, in person as much as an economic competitor. And if their trading practices make it easier to do so, then apparently so be it. The Trump outlook depicts global supply chains as taking jobs away from America, calling into question the logic on which global business has relied on for years. Muscular use of tariffs constricts the hitherto generous access to the US economy. Financial policies and social pressures are seeking to bring manufacturing back to America. There are moves afoot to also 'decouple' the Western world from China in the sphere of sensitive technologies. How much they will succeed remains to be seen.

The other driver of the current volatility is opposition to global mobility. The phenomenon itself is a consequence of the spread of skills and more efficient economic practices. However, difficult times are increasing hostility to its social aspects. After all, cultural insularity goes hand in hand with economic protectionism. But these pressures must contend with business realities that have developed deep roots.

All said and done, talent will remain the prerequisite for technology leads. And this is what can make India's position very different. It is the only viable reservoir that prepares skills before they flow into the world economy. The economic merits of such adjustable sources trump their social and political aspects. Making itself more relevant to the global knowledge economy clearly holds the key to India's future relationships.

The impact on the global order of these developments is likely to be visible over the next generation. That would have many dimensions, each of them in itself a source of potential instability. The most obvious one is that the world will be increasingly multipolar as distribution of power broadens and alliance discipline dilutes. An India or a Brazil will demand a greater voice with a growing economy. Germany and Japan cannot be impervious to change in American thinking on, say, Russia or Korea. As consistency starts to be questioned, many more nations will start to do their own thinking and planning.

A more nationalistic approach to international relations will undeniably weaken multilateral rules in many domains. This will be particularly sharp in respect of economic interests and sovereignty concerns. Undermining the working of the World Trade Organization or disregarding the Law of the Seas are not good signs. This prospect of multipolarity with less multilateralism suggests a more difficult future even for the near term. This does not mean giving up on the latter. On the contrary, it requires a new energy to be poured into reformed multilateralism. The current anachronistic order must be pushed to change, along with its outdated agenda.

It is also important to appreciate that the issue is not a binary choice between defending the order or inviting disorder. Unless we recognize that key elements of the order are no longer working for many stakeholders, confusion will continue to prevail over change. This will necessarily bring to the fore uncomfortable questions about current observance of rules, in both letter and spirit. And as major powers selectively advance arguments, much of the basic consensus that underpins the current reality will start to fray.

The emerging world is also likely to fall back on balance of power as its operating principle, rather than collective security or a broader consensus. History has demonstrated that this approach usually produces unstable equilibriums. World affairs will also see a proliferation of frenemies. They will emerge from allies who criticize each other or competitors compelled to make common cause. A more transactional ethos will promote ad hoc groupings of disparate nations who have a shared interest on a particular issue. This would be supported by requirements of working together and reaching out beyond alliance structures. The combination of these developments will encourage more regional and local balances with less global influence on their working.

The really uncharted territory that US-China frictions will take us into is that of coping with parallel universes. They may have existed before, most recently during the Cold War. But not with the inter-dependence and the inter-penetration of the globalized era. As a result, divergent choices and competing alternatives in many spheres will rest on partially shared foundations. This dilemma will be evident in a growing number of domains, from technology, commerce and finance to connectivity, institutions and activities. The key players will themselves struggle with the dichotomy of such parallel existence. Those who have to manage both, as most of us will, may then find themselves really tested.

Even if ties between China and the West take on a more adversarial character, it is difficult to return to a strongly bipolar world. The primary reason for that is the landscape has now changed irreversibly. Other nations are independently on the move, including India. Half of the twenty largest economies of the world are non-Western now. Diffusion of technology and demographic differentials will also contribute to the broader spread of influence. We see forces at play that reflect the relative primacy of local equations when the global construct is less overbearing. The reality is that the US may have weakened, but China's rise is still far from maturing. And together, the two processes have freed up room for others. Both have a use for third parties as they contest each other. In fact, their mutual dynamic may well drive multipolarity faster.

The beneficiaries could well be middle powers. Those who already have prior advantages like Russia, France and UK will get a new lease of life. Some like India can aspire to an improved position. Others, like Germany, would increase their weight through collective endeavours. But this will also be a world of a Brazil and Japan, of Turkey and Iran, a Saudi Arabia, Indonesia or an Australia, with a greater say in their vicinity and even beyond. The dilution of alliance discipline will only further facilitate this process. What will emerge is a more complex architecture, characterized by different degrees of competition, convergence and coordination. It will be like playing expanded Chinese Checkers including with some who are still arguing over the rules.

A multipolar world that is driven by balance of power is not without its risks. Europe, with its World War experiences, is especially chary. Even dominant powers – the US, Russia earlier or China now – favour such balancing only for specific contingencies and not as a general approach. Past experience does suggest that unchecked competition can often spiral downwards, both regionally and at the global level. For that reason, international relations envisage collective security as a safety net. Even if that did not always work, broader consensus through wider consultations functioned as a Plan B. Those most unsettled at the prospect of multipolarity with weaker rules are nations that have long functioned in an alliance construct. Unlike independent players, it is understandably difficult for them to accept that the compulsions of inter-dependence are a good enough substitute. Others may contemplate this prospect with greater nervousness; but an India perhaps with a more open mind.

An individualistic world means that the entrenched order is more open to newer players. Longstanding collective positions may become less rigid. That the format of play is also more bilateral strengthens the inclination to make accommodations. This has been particularly in evidence in the security domain. Whether it is the nuclear deal and the NSG waiver, the partnerships in Afghanistan or the Malabar Exercise, they reflect a departure from the old group think to more contemporary pragmatism. It could also now extend to other domains.

Friends who differ or competitors who cooperate are a notable trait of this emerging scenario. Both express different aspects of constraints that limit freedom of choices in an interdependent world. The rise of nationalism is largely responsible for the former group while global threats bring the latter together. Thus, we have seen the US differ with much of the Western world, especially Europe, on issues like climate change. The politics of the Trans-Pacific Partnership and the NAFTA were examples of the divisive role of trade. Energy policy has been an equally potent area, reflected in American criticism of Europe's dependence on Russia. But more than specific issues, frenemies have grown as mindsets have changed. The belief that alliances are burdensome is by itself a cause for frictions.

In the final analysis, the utility of the current dispensation to America's global posture has come into question. The momentum of the past, however, can still keep combinations alive of nations who may disagree about the present. Despite differences of views, traditions do continue a basis for working together, even if unhappily. A very different motivation is provided, however, by the compulsions of common concerns. We have seen coalitions of convenience on global issues like counterterrorism, maritime security, non-proliferation or climate change. These are issue-based and can again be effective even when grudging.

If division within alliances was one evolution, reaching beyond them was another. As the world moved in the direction of greater plurilateralism, result-oriented cooperation started to look more attractive. They were better focused and could be reconciled with contrary commitments. The growing imperative of sharing responsibilities was combined with an appreciation of influences beyond formal structures. Asia has been a particular focus for such initiatives, as regional architecture is the least developed there. India today has emerged as an industry leader of such plurilateral groups, because it occupies both the hedging and the emerging space at the same time.

Working with different powers on security, political and developmental issues has shown that making common cause can be extended by pragmatism and imagination. The twilight world is one full of partial agreement and limited agenda. Its ambiguous nature requires flexible arrangements that are customized to the challenge. These practices will not only become more widespread in coming times but occupy a prominent place in the foreign policy of states beyond India.

A world of multiple choices is increasingly opening up at different levels. We surely see that at the big table, where larger powers are dealing more opportunistically with each other. Through their behaviour, they encourage the rest of the world to also do so. In the light of the global balance being so fluid, the shaping of the local one has become a subject on its own. In the Gulf, there is a multi-cornered contest underway with faith, governance models, political principles and balance of power all providing variables. Less complex examples litter other parts of the world.

As they throw up issues, it is more effective for India to respond with engagement than by distancing. The skill that current diplomacy values most is dealing with contesting parties at the same time with optimal results. The pressure on players is definitely more in a higher intensity and less structured game. But there is a reason why going up the global power hierarchy is judged by the ability to successfully manage conflicting priorities.

Dominating the global stage today is very different from earlier days. When the world was much simpler, so too was the rise of powers. Fortunes were made and unmade by a combination of national strength, international opportunities and the quality of leadership. Superior technologies and practices produced decisive outcomes, often on the battlefield. Today, the variables that drive power and affect calculations are many more. Their interplay is also complex and less predictable. Equally important, their application takes place in a constrained, globalized and interdependent world. As a result, accumulation of influence substitutes for much rawer exercises of strength. Strategy has become more an effective deployment of resources than the use of force. Technology has opened up options like weaponization of finance or cyber interventions.

At the same time, persuasion and incentives are also more common than coercion. Consequently, nations now rise in a different way, without necessarily a signature moment of transformation. The global financial crisis of 2009 is a telling example where neither China, the rising power, nor the US, the one yielding ground, fully appreciated at that time the enormity of the tipping point.

An increase in the influence of nations may be more diffused and perhaps less tangible. But nevertheless, it is equally real. No one doubts China's influence on the world stage, even if they don't ponder that it was achieved by running trade surpluses rather than by shedding blood. Financial instruments, displays of strength and connectivity projects have provided opportunities to assert power without physically clashing with competitors.

That said, the latent threat of growing capabilities continues to underpin hard power. It explains why some, for example, embellish their past conflicts so much. In the case of India too, maintaining a more robust military posture and carrying out the

1998 nuclear tests were essential milestones in its evolution. But its global image is equally the result of its response to the Y2K challenge, its higher rate of growth and global acquisitions by its business. Power itself has now come to have different attributes and not all of them reside in the same nation.

The US, for example, remains the world's technological leader by a long stretch. But while behind on this score, China has used its financial and trading muscle to carve out for itself the number two slot. Europe is highly regarded for its industrial strength and quality of products. Even though it has pursued interventionist policies beyond the continent, it is still seen as punching below its weight. In contrast, Russia has summoned up its longstanding capabilities and by sheer willpower reinvented itself as a key player. So, what is the global hierarchy of power is no longer an easy question to answer. Because it has so many facets and is played out more locally, we are back to the matrix of many sides, many players, many games.

The domain most affected by all these disruptions is the provision of global goods. American parsimony and Chinese nationalism have renewed a debate on this subject. The vision and activities of Europe have also shrunk. Few other powers have moved to pick up the slack, India being a part exception. An unwillingness to commit resources to a larger global cause is very much in consonance with a narrower approach to international relations. That debate is framed, for example, around continuing troop commitments to Afghanistan and the Middle East. Or responding to the corona pandemic more lately. But it is much more complicated than that, encompassing respect for international law or responding to serious misbehaviour. Indifference to the most egregious actions of terrorism, for example, allowed it to become the norm in a large geography. India, of course, has a particular complaint in that context.

The discipline of the global order was given credit in the past for a range of preventive measures. Non-proliferation experts would confirm that many more nations would have gone nuclear but for alliance pressures. Much has depended on the credibility of key powers in underwriting their commitments. If that erodes, it could have a profound impact on the calculations of many. It will also make it difficult to reach understandings on new dimensions of threat, such as in cyber or space. The next decade will unfortunately be less generous and so more unsafe.

Keeping that in mind, India has to carefully navigate the near future whose contours are starting to define themselves. Leading nations, not just the US and China, will be surely more nationalistic and create space for others. Power distribution will continue to spread and multipolarity will accelerate. But greater players will not mean better rules; probably quite the opposite. As new capabilities and domains rise, global rules will struggle to keep pace. These developments will pose challenges to a rising power like India that would definitely prefer greater predictability. But if it can handle the uncertainty, its rise can also be faster.

At various levels of global politics, balances of power will be sought and often achieved. Loose and practical arrangements of cooperation will proliferate across geographies. Some will be composed of the like-minded, others more opportunistic, and still more, a mix of the two. Regional politics and local balances will gain importance.

Clearly, India will have to engage a broader set of partners more creatively. The transactional bazaar will bring together frenemies, grappling with the compulsions of globalization. Many will use the newer techniques of finance, connectivity or technology. India will need to find adequate responses, nationally where possible or in partnership, where required. Each of these issues is a challenge in itself and their matrix will determine India's future in a volatile world.

India could rise in an incremental way, as it was hitherto wont to do, hoping to play a balancing role as new equations came into play. Or, it could be bolder and seek to determine agendas and outcomes. To some extent, Indian hesitations of playing a leading role derive from its recollection of formidable powers like the US and USSR. But China has shown that a developing society, albeit of a large size and dynamic economy, can start to assume that responsibility. India could well follow in its footsteps, obviously at its own pace. That is, in fact, the calculation or perhaps even hope in many quarters.

A flatter world has been beneficial to India as its rise has been welcomed by many entrenched powers. The American interest in working with India has been evident for two decades and has now further accelerated. Russia remains a privileged partner with whom geopolitical convergence is a key consideration even in shifting circumstances. That has given the relationship a unique ballast. After Brexit, a more uncertain Europe has also developed a growing interest in India as a force of stability and growth in Asia. China, for its part, sees India as inherent to the rise of Asia and the larger rebalancing of the power distribution. The expansion of Japan's concerns and interests has created the basis for a completely different quality of ties. Countries of Asia, especially in the ASEAN and the Indo-Pacific, visualize merits in India's ability to shape a more multipolar Asia. The other extended neighbourhood in the Gulf has also welcomed the return of India to its region. While doing all this, India has retained its traditional constituencies of support in Africa and the rest of the political South. As the power differential vis-à-vis the world narrows, collaboration possibilities have expanded. If the world has developed stakes in India's prominence, the latter, in turn, can utilize that sentiment to the fullest.

Improving economic and political prospects is the necessary condition to contemplate India's rise in the world order. But sufficiency requires a favourable environment as well as the leadership and judgement to take advantage of it. And it is changes in regard to these two factors that today make a strong case to take India's aspirations more seriously. The right strategic calculations require a proper comprehension of the transformation in the international landscape. Assessing its contradictions accurately at the global and regional level opens up opportunities for progress. At its heart right now is the dynamic between the US and China. But also relevant are the determination of Russia, the choices of Japan and the durability of Europe. The loose coalition of developing states will play some part, although it increasingly differentiates on issues of concern. And as multipolarity grows and discipline erodes, it is really sharper regionalism that can produce outcomes beyond the control of major powers. Multilateralism may well take a backseat as rules and norms come under greater scrutiny and the consensus among the Permanent Five (US, Russia, China, UK and France) weakens. All in all, this points to more fluidity and unpredictability.

In theory, this new reality should be welcomed by the beneficiaries. After all, the demand for a more multipolar world has been pressed for many years by them. Now that multipolarity is upon us, its compulsions and responsibilities will make themselves felt. Nations will have to forge issue-based relationships that can often be pulling them in different directions. Keeping many balls up in the air and reconciling commitments to multiple partners takes great skill. There will be convergence with many but congruence with none. Finding common points to engage with as many power centres will characterize diplomacy.

The country that fares the best is the one which has least problems with its peer group.

India must reach out in as many directions as possible and maximize its gains. This is not just about greater ambition; it is also about not living in yesterday. In this world of all against all, India's goal should be to move closer towards the strategic sweet spot.

The shifting sands of global politics have always been the determining context for national choices. The post-colonial era that followed the Second World War saw India's return to the international arena as a sovereign power. Gaining independence ahead of many other colonies, it enjoyed first-mover advantages in world affairs for a considerable period. The next shift came when India had to respond to the Sino-US rapprochement, one facilitated by Pakistan. It did so by aligning to a great degree with the USSR. While that too took it through the next few decades, economic compulsions and the onset of unipolarity compelled further adjustment. The Indo-US nuclear deal of 2005 was symbolic of this repositioning which helped accelerate India's rise in the global order. Today, this country finds itself at another crossroads, this time one where choices are less clear and risks more complicated. To forge ahead, it is imperative that there is an adequate appreciation of the enormity of the disruption to which the international system is now being subjected.

As Indians weigh their prospects, they must consider themselves in the overall flow of modern history. Placing national prospects in a context of global events does not come easily to self-absorbed societies. Yet, divorced from the larger picture, they could misread their position or ignore their destiny. India's current modernization is one of a series that goes back to the Meiji Restoration in Japan. Even then, Indian nationalists perceived it as the beginning of the revival of Asia, hailing

Japan's victory over Russia in 1905. But it was that country's socio-economic transformation that was the really lasting story. The creation of the Soviet Union, emergence of the 'tiger' economies in East Asia and the ASEAN, and, finally, the rise of China – all saw the rest of Eurasia playing catch-up. Each one of these developments have had their influence on India, sometimes unconsciously so. Admittedly, India is the only one to have undertaken this journey more arduously on a democratic vehicle. But politics and sociology aside, its efforts in the last quarter century reflect broadly similar goals and objectives as those of Asia. If it differed, it was more in the depth and intensity of change, where an evolutionary approach produced less sweeping outcomes. Some of the consequential constraints are therefore only now being addressed.

Foreign policy is now an exercise to assess the disruptions underway and the trends that accelerate, mitigate or counter new directions. The coronavirus pandemic may well be a further complicating factor. But as the global architecture opens up and India's own capabilities strengthen, it has greater freedom than in the past to organize its rise. This process will naturally have its risks that will need careful assessment. Much of the strategy would revolve around creating a more favourable landscape. Changing the global discourse in its favour is also essential at this time. But the end goal even, perhaps especially, in a volatile world is clear. Many friends, few foes, great goodwill, more influence. That must be achieved through the India Way.

3

Krishna's Choice

The Strategic Culture of a Rising Power

―――

'A nation that doesn't honour its past has no future'

― GOETHE

A multipolar world with frenemies, balance of power and a clash of values may today present a challenge for global politics. Yet, these were the very characteristics of a period in India that is captured by a particularly powerful epic. As India rises, questions will naturally be asked as to what kind of power it will be. If nothing else, the world's experience with China's rise will surely prompt such queries. It is also something that Indians should be asking of themselves. Part of the answer may well lie in India's own history and traditions.

Until recently, a Western paradigm has dictated global norms and values. China, as the first non-Western power to seriously rise in the post-1945 era, has drawn on its cultural heritage to project its personality and shape the narrative. It is but logical that India too should follow suit. Indeed, if there are today hurdles to understanding India's viewpoint, much of that arises from an ignorance of its thought processes. That is hardly surprising when much of the West was historically so dismissive of our society. It is revealing that the standard American introduction to Indian strategic thought does not even refer to the Mahabharata, though that epic so deeply influences the average Indian mind. Imagine commenting similarly on Western strategic tradition ignoring Homer's *Iliad* or Machiavelli's *The Prince*! Or on China, disregarding their equivalent, *Three Kingdoms*. If this happens to

India, it is less due to our oral tradition than our limited global salience till now. This needs to be rectified precisely because a more multi-cultural appreciation is one sign of a multipolar world. But also because many of the predicaments that India and the world face currently have their analogy in what is really the greatest story ever told.

Putting out explanations is integral to the process of ascending the global hierarchy. Often, India's rise is an issue framed in terms of whether it would be an Eastern or a Western power. Underlying this is a Eurocentric assumption that pluralism is a purely Western attribute. India, with a longer history of diversity and coexistence, defies that preconception. A second debate revolves around the themes of nationalism and globalism. Here too, India occupies a singular position in reconciling what others see as antithetical concepts. A nationalistic India is willing to do more with the world, not less.

But what perhaps distinguishes us from other traditions of statecraft is our approach to governance and diplomacy. India's history shows that it does not follow a 'winner takes all' approach to contestation. Nor is there a confident belief that the end justifies the means. On the contrary, the Indian narrative is interlaced with moderation and nuance that highlight the fairness of the outcomes. That reality may not have always lived up to such a standard does not invalidate these concepts. There is continuous reflection on both the goals and the processes, sometimes to the point of self-doubt. But what it boils down to is the importance of making the right choices in difficult situations.

The Mahabharata is indisputably the most vivid distillation of Indian thoughts on statecraft. Unlike the *Arthashastra*, it is not a compendium of clinical principles of governance. Instead, it is a graphic account of real-life situations and their inherent choices. As an epic, it dwarfs its counterparts in other civilizations, not just in length but in its richness and complexity. Focusing on the importance of the sense of duty and the sanctity of obligations, it is also a description of human frailties. The dilemmas of statecraft permeate the story, among them taking risks, placing trust, and making sacrifices. The courage required to implement policy is, perhaps, its most famous section – the Bhagavad Gita. But there are other elements of perennial politics as well, including tactical compromises, utilizing obsessive players, undertaking regime change and ensuring balance of power. Our current concerns have an ancient reflection in that tale, especially leveraging the external environment to address bilateral imbalances. The orthodoxies of strategic competition and gaming the system coexist with more contemporary concepts of controlling the narrative and valuing knowledge as power.

This is an account of debates and decisions made against the background of a competition that becomes a conflict. The global political situation now is nowhere that catastrophic. But it nevertheless has elements of similarity that hold lessons for decision-making now. The India of the Mahabharata era was also multipolar, with its leading powers balancing each other. But once the competition between its two major poles could not be contained, others perforce had to take sides. While there is no reason to suggest a literal repetition today, the manner in which costs and benefits were weighed by interested parties is instructive for all students of strategy. Like the landscape, the choices made then have some resemblance to our contemporary world. The more momentous of them is that of Sri Krishna, who provides strategic guidance, diplomatic energy and tactical wisdom in navigating challenges.

The best known of the dilemmas in the Mahabharata relates to a determination to implement key policies without being discouraged by the collateral consequences of the action. The example, of course, is that of the most accomplished Pandava warrior, Arjuna, as he enters the battlefield. Undergoing a crisis of confidence, he is unable to summon up the determination to take on kinfolk ranged against his interests. While he is eventually persuaded by Lord Krishna to do his duty, there are underlying aspects of Arjuna's behaviour that apply to state players in international relations. This is not to suggest disregard of cost-benefit analysis. But sometimes, even when there is a pathway, it may not be taken due to lack of resolve or a fear of costs.

Unlike Arjuna, we in India are less intimidated by comfort with the known, as by the fear of the unknown. In contemporary parlance, the expression 'soft state' describes a nation's inability or unwillingness to do what is necessary. In Arjuna's case, it was certainly not a situation of inability. And that, sometimes, is the predicament of the Indian state as well. In the longstanding fight against terrorism, for example, we are often constrained by our lack of imagination and fear of risks. That may have started to change, but it is important to match the level of resolve shown by others. Arjuna eventually takes the field as a righteous warrior and that sense of self-justification is important to recognize.

It is only when a national elite has a strong and validated sense of its bottom lines that it will take a firm stand when these are challenged. So, whether it is an issue of violation of sovereignty or infringement of borders, an ability to respond categorically can come from this inherent self-belief. Asserting national interests and securing strategic goals through various means is the dharma of a state, as indeed it was of an individual warrior. This needs underlining in a climate where judgements are sometimes made with the yardstick of popularity, rather than strategy.

Also relevant in this context is summoning the willpower to address concerns that are upon us, rather than rationalize inaction by highlighting its costs. We have heard, all too often, arguments that a competitor is too big to challenge and would anyway prevail in the end. Or, sometimes, that the very nature of a neighbour is to indulge in terrorism and we simply have to live with it. This is fatalism disguised as deliberation. If there is a message in Arjuna's choice, it is that we have to face up to responsibilities, however difficult their consequences. India's national security would have been significantly better if that had been more widely appreciated and practised.

One aspect where the strategic landscape at the time of the Mahabharata bears resemblance to our current world is in regard to the constraints that operate on competitors. In that era, these emanated from a range of human emotions, obviously very different from those that apply today. They were partly driven by a belief that conflict, by its very nature, is destructive to the interests of all the involved parties. There was therefore a visible reluctance to initiate it, among the Kaurava elders and even more, with King Yudhishtira. His brother Arjuna carries that feeling even into the battlefield. But this is also sharpened as sentiments from past relationships clash with the requirements of future interest. Both the patriarch Bheeshma and the teacher Drona display enormous reluctance to bring their full capability into play against their previous wards.

Today's constraints are less behavioural and more structural. Nuclear deterrence creates one threshold. Economic interdependence is probably a more compelling factor as markets react to tension, leave alone actual conflict. A more technological world is also more vulnerable, even if it has created greater capabilities. The range of options that were open earlier have steadily shrunk with the passage of time. In our own case, the scale of conflicts that took place earlier can no longer be realistically contemplated. While all polities will naturally plan for worst-case scenarios, the reality is increasingly of sharp responses, narrow windows and limited application. It does not do away with the need for building up strong overall capabilities. But it does shift the focus on the need to develop the mind games which are more relevant to the likely scenarios.

If there is one quality that a rising power must cultivate, it is that of displaying responsibility. The manner in which Arjuna finally took up arms at Kurukshetra not only highlighted devotion to duty; it also brought out his forbearance. He was, in that sense, a reluctant warrior. In a different way, so too was Sri Krishna. His willingness to forgive his cousin and rival Shishupala a hundred provocations before finally responding decisively is instructive. This too is a lesson for a nation with growing capabilities in the global arena. Power, especially as it grows, must be debated, projected and applied judiciously. Till now, India has rarely faced this dilemma. Most of the conflicts of our modern era have been defensive wars where their justification is largely self-evident. As events have shown in recent times, we need to cultivate the strategic patience required for modern day Shishupalas. India does not need irresponsible talk at this stage of its rise. Use of force must always be the considered option, never the first one. Even superpowers like the US discovered through their experience in Iraq the damage caused by the contrary approach. Major nations have multiple weapons in their armoury and blunt instruments are usually the least productive. But efficacy aside, the imagery is no less significant. Those who casually advocate application of force abroad do damage. Such actions, as the instructive epic tells us, are an option reserved for imminent danger or serial offenders.

Most strategists fight the last war, not the next. In that context, Arjuna made a consequential choice some time before the battle began. Both he and his rival-cousin Duryodhana went to Krishna's capital Dwarka to seek his support as an ally. Arjuna arrived later but was seen first by the awakening host as he sat at the foot of the bed. Asked to choose between Krishna's army or his personal participation without weapons, Arjuna surprised Duryodhana by opting for the latter. His understanding of the game-changing potential of Sri Krishna was clearly the basis for his decision.

There is a moral in this as we consider enhancing competitiveness in national security. Like most warriors, Duryodhana thought in an orthodox manner, while Arjuna also understood what was outside the box. Without neglecting the established areas of capability, it is vital that this nation prepare itself better for what awaits the world. That may be in areas like artificial intelligence, robotics and data analytics or sensing, advanced materials and surveillance. Particularly if leveraging others is central to success, it is imperative that a contemporary and informed assessment of capabilities is made. Arjuna understood what Sri Krishna was about; Duryodhana did not.

This was not just about getting the big picture wrong but actually not appreciating what is at hand. Duryodhana was oblivious to the significance of Sri Krishna; or else he would not have underestimated him for lack of weapons. Understanding the full value of capabilities is as important as building them. The Pandavas clearly scored better in both departments. Today, India not only needs to pay attention to the quality of cards that it has but also focus on how to play them well.

Relations between states, like policies within it, are based on rules and norms. Even if they are breached from time to time, there is always a larger societal expectation that exceptions will remain just that. All players use practices and traditions to advantage and the Mahabharata is no different. The archery teacher Drona takes the thumb of a talented student, Eklavya, as the ritual offering to the master since he could otherwise overshadow his favourite, Arjuna. The god Indra, disguised as a Brahmin, seeks the invulnerable armour and earrings of the

Kaurava general Karna after prayers as it is the one time of the day when he cannot refuse him a favour. Arjuna uses a reincarnated woman as a cover in battle, knowing full well that Bheeshma will not fire back because of gender sensitivity. In a world that is now riven with trade disputes, technology fights and connectivity differences, it may be of some consolation to recall that not playing by the rules has a long history. If some have gamed the system or seek unintended benefits, this is a path that others have trodden before.

The Mahabharata also holds numerous examples of violations of codes of conduct, some more flagrant than others. The main protagonist Duryodhana is killed literally with a blow below the belt. Of the successive Kaurava commanders, one is brought down using a woman warrior as a shield, the second attacked after laying down weapons and the third decapitated when digging his chariot wheel out of the ground. Well-laid rules of individual combat fall by the wayside as stakes mount. Arjuna's son Abhimanyu is attacked by multiple adversaries simultaneously, including from the rear. His own father, Arjuna, also breaches the code in assaulting Bhoorisvaras when engaged in a fight with his longstanding rival Satyaki. Such deviations provided the justification for the most terrible act of the conflict, the night-time slaughter of the sleeping victors by Drona's son Ashwathama at the end of the war in revenge against the manner of his father's killing.

These examples frame a debate on the merits of observing rules and the costs of violating them. Their more contemporary versions can be found in every geography across all eras. For all the constraints and limitations that rules impose, compliance and its appearance are very valuable in international relations. Serial violators are given little credit even when they comply, while an occasional disrupter can always justify a deviation. In many ways, that was the difference between the Kauravas and the Pandavas. The importance of adhering to international law, agreements and understandings is not a theoretical debate. Powerful nations are understandably reluctant to put their options and interests at the judgement of others. That could be the case with India too as it gains in power and stature. Nevertheless, the advantage of being perceived as a rule-abiding and responsible player cannot be underestimated. We saw that when it came to accommodate nuclear aspirations, the world was far more trusting of India than Pakistan. This continues even further as they seek membership of key technology export control regimes. On a matter like maritime claims, India's acceptance of an arbitral award regarding Bangladesh in 2014 contrasted with what happened to the South China Sea one in 2016.

Playing by the rules is at the heart of games that nations indulge in with each other. To understand the mindset of others is often key to assessing how far they will go and from what they will shrink. The strength of an unorthodox player is to make an accurate judgement about the likely responses of the more orthodox and rule-bound one. While themselves indulging in unrestrained actions, their tactics would be to hold the other side to higher standards. Arbitraging that gap, of course, gives them a great edge. The final exchange between the rival brothers Karna and Arjuna is illustrative of this predicament, as indeed are the last moments of the Kaurava prince Duryodhana. Both Karna and Duryodhana expect competitors to live up to values that they have themselves flouted. Much of Sri Krishna's relevance to the Pandavas is his contribution to resolving these dilemmas and addressing the situations when rules stop being a rule.

In the modern world, open societies confront such challenges when going up against less scrupulous competitors. Fighting the uneven fight is their karma. The most extreme situations arise when confronting terrorism, especially that backed by state powers. As others have discovered before, there are no easy answers. Consider the diplomatic engagement between India and Pakistan in the last two decades. Pakistan indulges in nuclear scare-mongering to create a moral equivalence between a terrorist and a victim. We then make the mistake at Havana and Sharm-El-Sheikh of playing along. In this logic, 'strategic restraint' apparently applies only to the victim, not to the perpetrator. In fact, a narrative was even created that suggests there are no escalatory dangers when Pakistan commits terrorism, but only when India responds to such acts.

What is amazing is how many have bought this self-serving logic, expecting that India must naturally conform to it. Making it a game for two has, therefore, been a real challenge. The value of the Uri and Balakot responses was that, finally, Indian policy could think for itself rather than let Pakistan condition its answers. And that, in many ways, was the role of Sri Krishna as well on the Pandava side.

While deviations from the norm are less rare, a more complex issue is the role of deception. It clearly cannot be that activities in the domains of foreign policy and national security should be transparent in all respects. After all, incentives, fear and manipulation are part of human nature. Indian strategic thought, most notably Kautilya's writings, underline the importance of 'Sama, Dana, Danda and Bheda' (alliance, compensation, force and trickery) as the ways of approaching political challenges. The complexity of tactics grows in direct proportion to the gravity of the situation. We see that in two of the ethically disputable situations in the Mahabharata.

At a moment of battlefield desperation, the King Yudhishtira is persuaded to make a false public declaration to destroy the morale of Dronacharya, a critical opponent. Earlier, when

Arjuna's oath to kill an enemy by a deadline was being tested, Sri Krishna created an illusion of safety that encouraged Jayadratha, a hunted warrior, to expose himself with fatal consequences. In both cases, the letter of the action violated its spirit. Far more flagrant situations have happened in real life. Many of the most fateful battles in the modern world – Bosworth Field in England, Sekigahara in Japan or Plassey in India – have after all been decided by treachery. Sometimes, deception has even been justified as a call of honour, a case in point being the Japanese saga of the *47 Ronin*.

Yet, the world does seek conformity with rules and promotes observance of norms. For that reason, Japan sought to formally declare war just before attacking Pearl Harbour so that it was morally and technically in the right. Its failure to do so in time was enormously helpful to President Roosevelt in mobilizing political support. Narratives are necessary to justify departures and violations and each political culture produces its own version. In modern history, the British were probably the best in this business. Their storyline on India can go to the extent of suggesting that oppression was in the interest of the victim! Others have chosen their own mix of intentions and justification. Retaining the high moral ground is in many ways the ultimate test of realpolitik.

Strategic deception, by its very definition, is a high stakes initiative that requires a certain mindset to succeed. Usually involving a larger number of players and longer timelines, it is difficult to carry out without considerable internal discipline. In the Mahabharata, the Kauravas attempt it thrice against the Pandavas: once in seeking to drown Bheema, again in attempting to burn the Pandavas in a house of lac, and finally in inviting Yudhishtira to play a rigged game of dice. Authoritarian societies are intrinsically more skilled in this regard, and the correlation between statism and strategic deception in the modern world cannot be disregarded. While democracies are far from incompetent in this department, they do require strong and cohesive establishments to practice it effectively.

The Western experience has shown that such initiatives were easier to initiate and implement when there was unity of purpose. When it came to Russia, Yugoslavia, Libya or Syria, much has been done that was not spoken about. In contrast, there was a very divisive debate on Iraq that brought out many skeletons in many cupboards. Even the Afghanistan strategy has seen differences come to the fore on frequent occasions. One of India's challenges is that its sense of an establishment is not fully developed. Competitive politics is so visceral that perhaps the only continuity is that those in opposition can be counted on to oppose. This makes it very much harder to reconcile the gaps between narratives and intent.

The one society that has elevated dissimulation to the highest level of statecraft, as one of our foremost Sinologists[*] pointed out, is China. Its virtues are repeatedly lauded in the *Three Kingdoms* epic, where many of the decisive encounters are won by trickery rather than by force. The 36 Stratagems in the *Book of Qi* are further proof of how deeply such approaches have percolated into popular Chinese thinking. 'Deceiving the heavens to cross the ocean' or 'making a sound in the East to then strike West' are among its most well-known aphorisms. No less are 'decking trees with false blossoms' or the empty fort strategy. Unlike in India, there is neither guilt nor doubt in dissembling; in fact, it is glorified as an art. Some analysts[**] have

---

[*] Shyam Saran, 'China in the 21st Century', Second Annual K. Subrahmanyam Lecture, India International Centre, New Delhi, 2012.

[**] Michael Pillsbury, *The Hundred-Year Marathon* (New York: Henry Holt, 2015).

even suggested that China's extraordinary rise has drawn heavily on its cultural attributes.

India has, in contrast, struggled even with gaps between declared policy and actual objectives. Thus, in the 1950s, it was difficult to sustain the messaging of Asian brotherhood with China while preparing an effective border defence. With Pakistan, the nostalgia of a partitioned people has continuously competed with the reality of an obsessive adversary. Even in Sri Lanka, the mandate of peacekeeping was difficult to reconcile with the eventual application of force. Clearly, running a dual-track policy narrative with actual goals being at variance with stated positions is challenging in an environment when contradictions are publicly questioned. A more cohesive elite is best at overcoming this and successfully executing strategic deception. Those constrained by their inabilities can only take comfort in the reputational advantages that they inadvertently enjoy.

Among the critical players in the epic conflict who normally do not get adequate credit for their role are the Trigarta warriors led by Susarma, who hail from the Punjab of today. Traditional allies of the Kurus, they conceived a special enmity towards Arjuna, who defeated them while preparing the ground for Yudhishtira's coronation ceremony. Their single-minded hostility proved very dear to the Pandavas. Constantly pouring oil into the Kaurava fire, they collaborated in the effort to smoke the Pandavas out from the Virata kingdom during their period of exile. But most damagingly, it was their challenge to Arjuna of a fight to the death which diverted him away from the main battlefield to facilitate a Kaurava attempt at capturing his brother Yudhishtira alive. Arjuna does triumph, but this diversion leads to the death of Abhimanyu, his son, who alone could resist that Kaurava effort. The moral here is of the danger of smaller adversaries whose single-mindedness goes to the extent of destroying themselves to inflict damage.

The potential of such opponents, even if less suicidal, to cause grief should not be underestimated. Another relevant example is of the Sindhu king Jayadratha, who, after an earlier bruising encounter with the Pandavas, acquires the capability to take on the brothers minus Arjuna. As a consequence, he could single-handedly block the support that Abhimanyu expected from them once he entered the spinning wheel formation. In reality, such unifocal competitors are rare, but they deserve special attention once they become a fact of life. That, in many ways, sums up the predicament today of India vis-à-vis Pakistan.

Since 1971, that country has gone to extremes to hurt India even if its own system is corroded by the very forces it nurtures. India obviously cannot replicate Arjuna's solutions, but it does need to draw some appropriate lessons. Strategic clarity about Pakistan may well be a good starting point. The visceral feelings of such an adversary must be recognized. At the same time, neighbours are not a matter of choice, just as relatives were not in the Mahabharata. How does India straddle this dilemma?

There is no one-time fix and no Indian response should be judged by this impossible yardstick. It therefore will have to come up with its own set of answers. Ensuring that there are no longer guarantees of protection for terrorists is one such move. Enforcing accountability for acts of terrorism is another. Putting aside the naive expectation that engagement by itself is a solution is essential. Process can never be the remedy for behaviour. Pakistan's refusal to countenance normal trade or allow connectivity tells us much about its actual intentions. A practical response currently to such a posture, other than inflicting reputational damage, is to make that costly to sustain. Pakistan can only be treated as a normal neighbour when its behaviour corresponds to one. Till then, India will have to show a mix of fortitude, creativity and perseverance of a degree that would impress even Arjuna.

If choices of different nature each extract a cost, so do indecision, ambivalence and detachment. There are three contrasting approaches by players of eminence in this saga.

The first is of Shalya, the maternal uncle of the Pandavas, who is tricked by a false flag operation into committing to the Kaurava side. Yet, deception is a double-edged sword and his ambivalence ends up undermining the morale of the Kaurava general Karna, for whom he is the charioteer at a critical battle. Krishna's brother, Balarama, is genuinely neutral as he has taught warfare to both sides and opts out of the conflict by taking a long pilgrimage during the war. He comes back angered by its outcome and yet unable to influence it in any way. Rukmi of Vidharba is the other notable warrior who stays out of the war, but for a very different reason. He overestimates his value to both sides and ends up accepted by neither.

Each of these examples has some relevance in contemporary politics, especially for a nation that understandably has hedged on the big global divides. India's non-alignment policy has had different facets at various times, projecting some combination of these situations. Where we have remained uninvolved, we are nevertheless left to face the consequences. On some questions, we run the danger of displeasing all parties. Where we have aligned on larger contradictions, our reluctance in doing so fully has not been without costs.

Regime change has been in practice since states existed, even if it took the Iraq war in 2003 to bring it into the consciousness of the current generation. Because of its weak justification and messy consequences, that term is laden with negative connotations. Yet this practice has usually been justified on ethical considerations. In the Mahabharata, the most telling example was the killing of King Jarasandha of Magadha at the instance of Krishna. His removal was necessary to both put down an immediate challenge, as well as eliminate a focal point for larger opposition to Yudhishtira becoming emperor. From Krishna's viewpoint, it was also a settlement of a long outstanding score. What was noteworthy in this endeavour was its ostensible reason: the release of ninety-eight princes who were unjustly detained in Jarasandha's custody. There was even a situation of 'imminent danger', as he was threatening to sacrifice them when the number reached a hundred.

This also illustrates the value of what we would today call South-South cooperation, a coming together against the dominant. Assisting the vulnerable and weak clearly has great value in collective politics. Equally important, a national goal was attained in the name of global good. Regime changes are among the more controversial aspects of international relations since they are visibly violative of sovereignty. But if they must be done, it is best achieved with an ethical explanation that carries credibility. That may have been so in this particular case, but more recent examples like Iraq had less ring to their truth.

Leveraging the external environment is the other side of the coin of regime change. Here, the weaker player solicits or manipulates stronger forces to their advantage. There is no shortage of such situations as the conflict unfolds, bearing in mind that the military balance was 7:11 against the Pandavas. The very gods are invoked to acquire potent weapons and unorthodox capabilities. Building and maintaining alliances may be one avenue of influence, but accessing technology and utilizing knowledge of others is no less effective. This is particularly the case when up against stronger opponents, a strategic predicament to which India today needs to give more thought. Those who advocate strengthening comprehensive national power are certainly in the right; but that is the obvious answer. What should not be neglected is the skill to tap into the influence and power of others.

Modern history has telling examples of powerful nations who have failed just on this account. Wilhelmine Germany, for example, saw its poor diplomacy undermine what was a favourable power balance. Such skills are not just the requirement of the weak or the upwardly mobile. It is also the need of the powerful to retain constituencies of support and discourage collective reaction. Learning from errors is an associated skill so that mistakes are not repeated. One of the great ironies of the Mahabharata is that the same Yudhishtira who loses his kingdom in a game of dice becomes sufficiently skilled as to make it his employment later under King Virata.

Where the Pandavas consistently scored over their cousins was the ability to shape and control the narrative. Their ethical positioning was at the heart of a superior branding. Through acts of valour, nobility and generosity, they generally came out as the better side. Admittedly, they were victims on many occasions, but their ability to play victim was no less. Their very upbringing in the forest gives them a head start with public opinion. The attempt to kill them in the house of lac shows them as an injured party. Accepting an unfair partition of the kingdom fortifies that image. Successfully executing a start-up kingdom in Indraprastha adds to their lustre. The abominable treatment of their wife Draupadi gives them a casus belli that is never allowed to be dampened. The masterstroke was to make an offer of reasonable settlement and accepting just five towns on the eve of the war, so that peer opinion shifts in their favour.

There is a broad correlation between occupying the high moral ground and shaping the narrative. For that reason, during the Cold War, the two camps each put out their arguments vigorously. One stressed democracy, personal freedoms and market economy while the other emphasized social justice, common good and collective welfare. As China rose, it emphasized its peaceful character and underlined the larger prosperity implications. Developing nations improved their bargaining position by making a convincing case for positive discrimination in a wide range of activities. The Western world generally and the European Union specifically reinvented themselves by championing global issues and stressing the responsibility to protect. Much of that is in retreat today as narrower interests dominate current thinking and economic populism takes over. As China's capabilities expand, it may bring out the challenge of moving from the global to the universal. The US is moving the other way, diluting alliance commitments and going back on international obligations. In an ethos of strong national identities, India too will have to take a call on its own narratives. A society that would soon be the most populous and prominent in its economic size cannot be without its message. In the days when it was weaker, there was comfort in group mentality and non-involvement. That would be increasingly harder with the passage of time.

A subtext that runs through the Mahabharata is the balance of power among the kingdoms of India. Solidarity among them is often explained by kinship, but that itself is often an outcome of state interests. Two significant examples are the Panchala and Matsya kingdoms, the natural allies of the Pandavas. Stress situations are also helpful in revealing inherent leanings. Thus, while planning to hide out in the thirteenth year of their exile, the Pandavas identify kingdoms that would be friendlier. Similarly, when strategizing to take out Jarasandha, Krishna not only highlights his closeness to the Kauravas but lists other allied kingdoms who would be weakened by his elimination. In many ways, the battle lines on the Kurukshetra battlefield bring out the intricacies of a very complex matrix.

Today, that intuitive feel for creating and maintaining balances has perhaps diminished in our country. A variety of factors discouraged a deep dive into world politics that is so necessary for this exercise. Some of that reflects limitations in our own capacities. As that improves, so too should confidence levels. If we have reservations on balance of power, it is because the period leading up to the World Wars saw it degenerate into uncontrolled competition. The discipline of the Cold War also created rigidities which minimized the importance of such possibilities. As that ended, a widespread belief in interdependence and globalization obviated such thinking. All of these are now changing in an era of greater nationalism, flatter landscapes and diluted alliances.

The shift towards realpolitik also brings to the fore the costs and justification of policy prescriptions. Tragic though Abhimanyu's death was, in the larger scheme of things, it was collateral damage of an effort to secure his king. More deliberate perhaps was the action of his grandmother Kunti, who replaced her own family with a set of guests before setting the house of lac on fire. Or the sacrifice of Arjuna's son Iravan as a price to be paid for victory when the war started. Maybe less conscious during the battle was the death of the nephew Ghatotkacha to Karna's unstoppable shakti weapon, thereby precluding its possible use against his uncle Arjuna. National interest has operational costs and making those decisions is often the most difficult responsibility of leadership.

The Pandavas are an excellent example of integration. Born of different mothers and each with a complex paternal origin, they function very well as a team overcoming internal tensions. They have complementary skill sets that make the combination particularly effective. As a model, they should inspire greater deliberation on the difficulties of working together efficiently. India has more than its fair share of this problem because we are blessed with both social pluralism and extreme individualism. Overlaid with the reality that there has been limited administrative reform, the need for greater integration is really very strong. Jointness, coordination and sharing are connected challenges of all large organizations. They grapple with set habits, vested interest and distinct identities. Agreeing at the headlines level rarely leads automatically to it working out operationally. Some of it may be conscious, but history and experience do pull in the opposite direction. Indeed, other than building better capabilities, breaking silos is as close as one can come to a silver bullet in the field of policy implementation.

If we in India have acquired a reputation for operating with sub-optimal coordination, it is because our history is replete with examples that came at great cost. Individualism could be aggravated by a possessiveness which has been enhanced by shortages. Bureaucratism has also been entrenched in our society. What perhaps adds to all of this is a focus on process rather than concern over outcomes. The lack of integration comes in different forms, but it is only by attacking them in all their manifestations that Indian foreign policy can really change for the better.

The Mahabharata is a saga of approaches and choices whose cumulative impact propels the polity in a certain direction. Each of them holds some lesson for the current times. The Kauravas, most notably, push competition to its extreme limits, creating a backlash that even justifies the emulation of their abominable tactics. The Pandavas, in contrast, build brand and display strategic patience. As a result, they are able to defeat a superior adversary, in part by the use of asymmetric tactics. Karna represents alliance discipline at its best, highlighting the impact of polarization. Bheeshma and Drona may stand with the establishment, but their ambivalence costs their side dear. This is in contrast to Drupada, whose single-mindedness enhances his value as an ally. The

Trigarta, as noted earlier, are its more extreme version. Shalya, Balarama and Rukma are the spectrum of non-alignment to non-involvement. And as for Kunti, her emotional commitments do not preclude a willingness to pay the operational costs of success.

The determining factor, as we all know, is Sri Krishna. He understands the big picture, fashions a strategy accordingly and comes up with tactical solutions at decisive moments. His choices set the direction, whether it is in structural change, shaping sentiment, enhancing brand or creating narratives. By bringing down Jarasandha, he is able to ensure a more favourable balance of power. Whether it is through his own presence or by the sagacious advice tendered, he helps swing opinion in favour of the Pandavas. His diplomatic overtures underline the message of a reasonable power, thereby making his side look the injured party. At key moments – the killings of Jayadratha, Karna or Duryodhana – he is both the motivator and the justifier. He is also the advocate of restraint to the Pandavas, encouraging them to bide their time and acquire the necessary capabilities for a conflict that is inevitable. His may be the voice of reason or the words of caution, but equally it is also the call to action when required. It is not just that he shows the pathway when others flounder. Most important, he does the right thing with full responsibility.

The Mahabharata is as much a tale of ethics as of power. It is Sri Krishna's choices that reconcile these two imperatives. As Indians prepare for greater contributions, they must rely on their own traditions to equip them in facing a tumultuous world. That is certainly possible in an India that is now more Bharat. As we make our choices in a world of all against all, it is time to come up with our own answers. Being an ethical power is one aspect of the India Way.

4

The Dogmas of Delhi

Overcoming the Hesitations of History

———

'History is the version of past events that people have decided to agree upon'

— NAPOLEON BONAPARTE

Albert Einstein is best known for his theory of relativity. Had he opted for a career in political science, he could have as easily been famous for a theory of insanity. His definition of that state of mind was doing the same thing over and over again – and expecting different results. A corollary of that is to do the same thing in different situations – and then expect the same results. This is important to recognize at a moment in world politics when many of our long-held beliefs no longer hold true. If the world is different, we need to think, talk and engage accordingly. Just falling back on the past is unlikely to help in preparing for the future.

The world is not just different; the very structure of the international order is undergoing a profound transformation. American nationalism, the rise of China, the saga of Brexit and the rebalancing of the global economy are often cited as the more dramatic examples of change. In fact, the phenomenon is far more pervasive than just these illustrations. We have seen a return of old empires like Russia, Iran or Turkey through greater energy and influence in proximate regions. West Asia is in ferment, even by its exceptionally volatile standards. The centrality of ASEAN to Asia is not what it is used to be. Demographic and economic trends in Africa are giving that continent a greater salience. South America is once again a battleground for ideas.

But we are also talking beyond geographies and orthodox politics. What defines power and determines national standing is no longer the same. Technology, connectivity and trade are at the heart of new contestations. In a more constrained and interdependent world, competition has to be pursued perforce more intelligently. The global commons is also more in disputation as multilateralism weakens. Even climate change is a factor, contributing to geopolitics by the opening of an Arctic passage. And the corona pandemic has been a wild card beyond all expectations. In short, change is upon us as never before.

If the landscape looks very different today, so too do India's key partners. The relevance of the US or China is far more than anytime earlier. The Russian relationship may have defied odds by remaining incredibly steady. But it is the exception, not the rule. Japan has now become an important factor in our calculations. The rediscovery of Europe is also underway, with France now a critical strategic partner. The Gulf has been bridged in an extraordinarily effective manner. ASEAN has grown closer, and Australia's relevance is more apparent. A strong sense of the extended neighbourhood is apparent. Africa is the focus of development assistance and opening of new Embassies. And as evident from diplomatic activities, our outreach extends from South America and the Caribbean to the South Pacific and Baltics. Closer home, there is an unprecedented investment in the neighbourhood whose consequences are becoming apparent. Put together, the scale and intensity of our global engagement would be difficult to recognize for someone dealing with it even a few years ago.

As the issues and relationships become different, so too will the argumentation. So, the first caution is to avoid obsessing about consistency, because it makes little sense in such changing circumstances. There is certainly a place for constants, but not to the extent of elevating them to immutable concepts. On the contrary, it is only by recognizing change that we are in a position to exploit opportunities. The purposeful pursuit of national interest in shifting global dynamics may not be easy; but it must be done. Prejudices and preconceptions cannot be allowed to stand in the way. And the real obstacle to the rise of India is not any more the barriers of the world, but the dogmas of Delhi.

An ability to respond to a variety of situations is part of any nation's rise. But most agents of change encounter the accumulated 'wisdom' of the entrenched, or the passionate argumentation of the polarized. In India, we also meet an obsession with words and text. Form and process are often deemed more important than outcomes. Fortunately, discontinuous politics is helpful today in challenging past practices and frozen narratives. It does so taking into account the steady elements of any policy; in India's case, a persistent striving to expand space and options. Not an end in itself, that is meant to ensure greater prosperity at home, peace on the borders, protection of our people and enhancing influence abroad.

Obviously, our national strategy, to realize even the more constant goals, cannot be static in an evolving world. We know that well, having seen the world move from bipolarity to unipolarity and now to multipolarity. But changes in strategy also need to cater for greater capabilities, ambitions and responsibilities. And most of all, for changed circumstances. In approaching such a world in transformation, we must recognize that assumptions need to be regularly revisited and calculations frequently revised. To do that, an accurate reading of recent history is essential. That exercise by itself can encourage appreciating the compulsions of responding to the environment, rather than mechanically applying doctrines and concepts.

Evidence strongly supports the view that India advanced its interests effectively when it made hard-headed assessments of contemporary geopolitics. And even more so as it did not hesitate, when demanded by challenges, to break with its own past. The 1971 Bangladesh war, the 1992 economic and political repositioning, the 1998 nuclear tests or the 2005 India-US nuclear deal are instructive examples. Indeed, it is only through a series of disruptions that India was able to bring about decisive shifts in its favour. In contrast, the pursuit of an apparently consistent course despite changing circumstances often led it to lose the plot. This was the case with engaging China in the 1950s as part of a larger post-colonial front, even as political differences sharpened over a boundary dispute and a Tibet complication. The experience with Pakistan was similar, despite that country progressively moving to greater reliance on terrorism. To some extent, this is a debate about realism and hard security. What it really suggests is a need for an unsentimental audit of Indian foreign policy.

India's record includes dark moments like the 1962 defeat against China. Or tense ones like the 1965 war with Pakistan, where the outcome hung in balance till the very end. And the more triumphal ones such as the 1971 victory which created Bangladesh. There are enough dichotomies in our past to generate a spirited debate on successes and failures. A misreading of geopolitics and economics up to 1991 stands in contrast to the reformist policies immediately thereafter. Two decades of nuclear indecision ended dramatically with the tests of 1998. The lack of response to 26/11 is so different from the Uri and Balakot operations.

Whether it is events or trends, they all bear scrutiny for the lessons they hold. If we look back at this journey of independent India, the growth in its capabilities and influence should not conceal the missed chances and shortcomings. The roads not taken may often be an exercise in imagination. But equally, they are a sign of honest introspection. A power that is serious about self-improvement should not shrink from such an undertaking.

How has Indian foreign policy evolved since Independence? Understanding that is done best by dividing into six phases, each a response to a different global strategic environment. The first phase, from 1946 to 1962, could be characterized as an era of optimistic non-alignment. Its setting was very much of a bipolar world, with camps led by the US and the USSR. India's objectives were to resist the constraining of choices and dilution of its sovereignty as it rebuilt its economy and consolidated its integrity. Its parallel goal, as the first of the decolonized nations, was to lead Asia and Africa in a quest for a more equitable world order. This was the heyday of Bandung and Belgrade, the peak of Third World solidarity. It also saw energetic Indian diplomacy from Korea and Vietnam to Suez and Hungary. For a few years, our position on the world stage seemed assured. The 1962 conflict with China not only brought this period to an end, but in a manner that significantly damaged India's standing.

The second phase, from 1962 to 1971, is a decade of realism and recovery. India made more pragmatic choices on security and political challenges while addressing a paucity of resources. It looked beyond non-alignment in the interest of national security, concluding a now largely forgotten defence understanding with the US in 1964. External pressures on Kashmir, especially from the US and UK, mounted in this period of vulnerability. The global context remained bipolar, but it now saw the emergence of limited cooperation between the US and USSR. South Asia happened to be a particular area of convergence and Indian diplomacy had to face the superpowers together, as it did in 1966 in Tashkent. It was also a period when domestic challenges were particularly acute, ranging from political turbulence to economic distress. But for our purposes, what is important is that even though the stress levels were higher, we came through an anxious period without great damage.

The third phase, from 1971 to 1991, was one of greater Indian regional assertion. It started with the decisive dismantlement of an India-Pakistan equivalence through the creation of Bangladesh, but ended with the IPKF misadventure in Sri Lanka. The larger environment by now was dramatically different, with the Sino-US rapprochement of 1971 upending the strategic landscape. The Indo-Soviet Treaty and the adoption of more pro-Soviet positions on international issues were India's response to this challenge. It was a particularly complex phase as the US-China-Pakistan axis which came into being at this time seriously threatened India's prospects. While there were many long-term consequences from it, the shift in India's posture arose more from other factors. The collapse of the USSR, its close ally, and the not-unconnected economic crisis in 1991 compelled us to look again at the basics of both domestic and foreign policy.

The dissolution of the USSR and the emergence of a 'unipolar' world characterized the fourth phase. It encouraged a radical rethink in India on a broad range of issues. And it shifted focus to safeguarding strategic autonomy. If India opened up economically more to the world, its reflection was also evident in new diplomatic priorities and approaches. The Look East policy summarized the changed Indian approach to world affairs, which also saw adjustments in its position on Israel.

This is a period where India reached out to engage the US more intensively, yet it did so while protecting its equities in critical areas. This quest for strategic autonomy was particularly focused on securing its nuclear weapon option, but also visible in trade negotiations. By the turn of the century, enough had happened for India to now shift gear again and move to a higher level. After 1998, it was now a declared nuclear weapon power, had fended off Pakistan's military adventurism again at Kargil in 1999, generated enough economic growth to be of global interest, and managed well a US that was focusing more on developments in Asia and the consequences of Islamic fundamentalism.

This more competitive environment opened up new windows of opportunity for India, especially as the US found it difficult to maintain the same degree of unipolarity. As a consequence, India discovered the benefits of working with different powers on different issues. This fifth phase is one where India gradually acquired the attributes of a balancing power. Its relevance to the world increased, as did its ability to shape outcomes. It is reflected in the India-US nuclear deal as well as a better understanding with the West. At the same time, India could also make common cause with China on climate change and trade, and consolidate ties with Russia while helping to fashion BRICS into a major forum. This was, in some senses, again a period of opportunity where India moved the global needle by taking new positions.

A number of developments came together to change calculations by 2014, initiating the sixth phase. To begin with, China gathered more momentum and the terms of engagement it offered to the world progressively hardened. Balancing works best during a period of transition and was, therefore, inevitably mitigated as new realities took root. At the other extreme, the American trumpet sounded uncertain. US resource limitation was aggravated by risk aversion in the aftermath of the Iraq war. Declaring an Afghan withdrawal and displaying growing tepidity in the Asia-Pacific sent messages well beyond the immediate issues. For its part, Europe turned increasingly inwards, not appreciating that political agnosticism would have its own cost. Japan's efforts to acquire a greater say continued to unfold only gradually. The full impact of the 2008 financial crisis and global economic rebalancing also made itself felt in a variety of ways. As the world saw a wider dispersal of power and more localized equations, it was evident that multipolarity was now seriously upon us. Clearly, this called for a very different approach than practising politics with a more limited set of dominant players.

Faced with these developments and assessing the state of global regimes and coalitions, India chose to turn to more energetic diplomacy. It did so recognizing that we were now entering a world of convergences and issue-based arrangements. This awareness was accompanied by a growing sense of its own capabilities. What it has brought out is not just the limitations of others, but the expectations the world has of India. That we have emerged among the major economies of the world is one factor, though admittedly the most important. The relevance of our talent to global technology is another, one likely to grow. Our ability to shoulder greater responsibilities at a time when the world is more reticent is also evident. Equally significant is a willingness to shape key global negotiations, such as in Paris on climate change. The investment of greater resources in development partnerships with countries of the South is also noteworthy. And not least, the manner in which we have approached our own region and the extended neighbourhood has resonated beyond.

Each of the six phases have had their highs and lows. The ending of one could be the beginning of another. The 1971 Bangladesh war or the 1998 nuclear tests stand out in the positive category. But the negative ones perhaps were more directly responsible for substantial changes of course. The 1962 reverse against China was one example. The combination of events as diverse as the Gulf War, the break-up of the USSR, economic stagnation and domestic turbulence coming together in 1991 was another. Therefore, while not being dogmatic about the past, it is just as important not to be dismissive about it either. This is crucial to appreciate because there are both strains of continuity and change in our policy. Conceptually, each period could be visualized as the overlay on the previous one, rather than either a negation or an extrapolation. Thus, the independent mindset that drove non-alignment and then protected our strategic equities can today be better expressed in multiple partnerships.

Seventy years of foreign policy certainly offer a lot of lessons, especially as we contemplate a challenging road ahead. They span a broad spectrum, both in time and in outcomes. A dispassionate assessment of our performance would note that while some competitors have done better, we have ourselves done not too badly. Overcoming many challenges, India consolidated its national unity and integrity. That was not a given, noting that some other diverse societies like USSR and Yugoslavia did not make it. A modern economy with industrial capacities was developed over time, even as our reliance on nature was mitigated in agriculture. Defence preparedness was improved and one of the key accomplishments of diplomacy was to enable access to multiple sources of equipment and technology.

However, the fact remains that even after seven decades of independence, many of our borders remain unsettled. In the economic sphere, we may look good when benchmarked against our own past. It seems a little different when compared to China or South-East Asia. So what really matters is to develop a sharp awareness about our own performance. An evaluation is helpful in developing that but must, in fairness, be set against the context of its era.

Since a fierce independence runs as a thread through our policy evolution, it is perhaps useful to begin with an updated understanding of what non-alignment was all about. Until the 1962 conflict, India's effort was to get the best from the two camps that the Cold War had created. It was successful in obtaining economic and food assistance from the West, while simultaneously seeking collaboration in industrialization from the Soviet bloc. For its security needs, India approached both with some success, eventually getting adequate capabilities from the USSR.

In different ways, China too attempted the same, although with greater ambition and less consistency. Indeed, the steadiness of one contrasted with the disruptiveness of the other. It is an open question whether one could have adopted the approach of the other; perhaps they were statements of their character. The middle path was not just a policy choice for India; it also reflected contradictory structural pulls. With the West, India was bound by a broad network of post-colonial economic, social and political linkages; but Cold War pressures prevented excessive closeness. With the USSR, the planned economy model and industrial aspirations generated an enthusiasm that was balanced against pluralistic political beliefs. As India went about the task of consolidating its national integration, both camps served its interests at different points of time. Most important, they helped expand its political space at a time when a large number of nations were regaining their freedom. This allowed India the leadership opportunity to build its own constituency and brand through the 1950s.

Broad concepts are not always easy to translate into policy, interests and outcomes. Non-alignment was no exception to the rule. India's engagement with the West was heavily Eurocentric and did not cater adequately for the new American primacy. This contrasted with the determined cultivation of the new superpower by the Pakistani elite. Differences with the US in the larger global arena also helped solidify American support for Pakistan, to a point where that country eventually reached a tactically superior position in 1965. At the other end, the political opening with the USSR provided early harvest, including support in the UN on Jammu and Kashmir. Its defence dimensions took more time to unfold. But the USSR's ideological linkages with China continued even when under strain, thereby limiting its role in the 1962 events.

In an interesting way, non-alignment also impacted the bilateral-multilateral balance of Indian diplomacy. The pursuit of a global profile sometimes came at the cost of narrower national interests. Eventually, an obvious exercise in increasing international influence ended up as a fatal diversion. The commitment of key players to UN duty in 1960 during Nehru's visit to Pakistan and again in 1962 as the China front deteriorated spoke volumes on Indian priorities. The moment of truth, of course, was the 1962 conflict itself. Both its preparations and actual conduct affirmed the inadequacy of India's understanding of power.

We tend to assume that the events in the period leading up to 1962 were predestined. In fact, the narrative of a 'betrayal' was designed to mitigate responsibility for a policy disaster at the highest levels. It took such deep root that the subsequent demonization of China has stood in the way of an objective analysis of India-China relations in this period. Independent of the justification for boundary claims, there are some issues that need to be addressed in the context of India's larger posture vis-à-vis China.

There was a genuine debate within the Indian system whether in the aftermath of the 1950 Chinese move into Tibet we should have initiated steps to finalize what had now become a common border. This is not an entirely hypothetical issue because serious suggestions to this end were made by very senior policymakers. Sardar Patel's famous letter to Prime Minister Nehru was part of this internal discourse. However, in what presumably was a desire to avoid immediate friction, the decision made was to postpone such engagement. At that time, China was more isolated internationally and its own position on Tibet had not hardened as it did after 1959. More than the issue itself, what comes out is a tendency to postpone a difficult issue. Avoiding hard choices was true in respect of the nuclear option as well. The same mindset led to the limited involvement of the military leadership in decision-making during the 1962 conflict. Instead, at the first sign of setback, we turned to others for both advice and assistance.

From 1962 for a full decade, India made a hard-headed comeback, even if ground was retrieved only partially. Domestically, India sought to overcome the shock of its defeat and resisted territorial concessions to Pakistan in Jammu and Kashmir as the price to be paid to the West for its assistance. Political instability, including succession processes, added to economic distress arising from the failure of monsoons. A number of domestic political agitations – from Tamil Nadu to Punjab – undid the message of stability achieved in the first years of independence. Not entirely inappropriately, our nation was seen to have entered a 'dangerous decade'. The world itself was still very much bipolar but the two superpowers now had a common interest in working to check China. Significantly, India was one of the key focal points of this shared endeavour. While the China front remained relatively stable for India – not least because that country slid into the Cultural Revolution – the Pakistan one became increasingly dangerous, culminating in the 1965 conflict. The superpower condominium was very much at work in forcing on India a difficult compromise at Tashkent. Economic difficulties aggravated and American pressures mounted on the Vietnam question as India also saw a Soviet overture to Pakistan that represented its reading of the subcontinental reality. This period came to a head with two extraordinary events of realism that were cause and consequence.

The first was the Sino-US rapprochement of 1971 that was achieved with the facilitation of Pakistan and fundamentally altered the global strategic scenario. The second was a response of two directly affected parties that came in the form of an Indo-Soviet Treaty. For India, it represented a compromise between non-alignment and strategic security. The precipitating factor was, of course, the decisions of a Pakistani leadership that eventually led to a conflict with India. It is tempting to speculate whether India would have taken such a tough call in the headier days of international diplomacy. While we will never know, the fact is that its victory in the 1971 Bangladesh conflict represented a partial recovery from the reverses of 1962. More important, by breaking the equivalence with Pakistan, India ushered in a phase of greater regionalism.

This period, in fact, countered the pre-1962 tendency and should be valued for that, perhaps even more than the outcomes themselves. The willingness to expand the initial conflict beyond Jammu and Kashmir in 1965 was one example. This was not a scenario that Pakistan had prepared for adequately. Standing one's ground against a Pakistani force with superior arms was another. In both 1965 and 1971, the military was given more space and greater say, leading to better outcomes on both occasions. This was also the case with responding in Nathu La in 1967. In 1971, there was additionally much better strategizing in preparation for the use of force, including what at that time was a radical measure of concluding a treaty with the USSR. If there are lessons from the two contrasting periods for the present day, it is both of greater horizontal integration in the Indian national security system and of thinking through a response to an unavoidable challenge.

The following phase, starting with a decisive outcome on the battlefield, began in 1971. The division of Pakistan itself had profound consequences that are not lost on the rest of the region. In an unintended way, the half-hearted attempts by the US and China to assist Pakistan during the conflict only added to India's prestige. Yet, it is in the nature of a power to steadily broaden horizons and that is precisely what India did in its aftermath. Within a short space, there was an attempt to improve ties with the US, leading to a visit by Henry Kissinger in 1973. Kissinger himself was more than aware that this was an attempt to restore the balance after the events of 1971. The American response to India's 1974 nuclear test was, therefore, surprisingly sober. More difficult for India was the decision in 1976 to normalize ties with China and send back an Ambassador after a gap of fifteen years. Both could be seen as expanding its options. The broadening of its vision was also visible in the effort to create a third option in Europe. The acquisition of Jaguars, Mirages and HDW submarine were evidence of this hedging. Prime ministerial visits to the US in 1982 and 1985 as well as the tentative resumption of defence cooperation – involving the Light Combat Aircraft – were further indications. With China, boundary talks resumed in 1981 and reached a point of leadership-level discussions in 1988.

The real impact of India's enhanced stature was felt most in the immediate neighbourhood. The most important challenge was Pakistan, and in 1972 at Shimla, India chose to be generous. It was not that there was an absence of international pressure, including from the USSR itself. There was also a natural desire to shape the direction of Pakistani politics. But given the cards it held, even contemporary observers were surprised at the outcome. It took some time for the negative implications to unfold, but even as they did, India's assertion of its interests was more forceful than in the past. A decisive move on the Siachen glacier dealt with a growing concern. With Sri Lanka, anxiety at the ethnic conflict was sought to be translated into a settlement guaranteed by India. That the initiative went wrong is a different matter; undertaking it in itself was an act of no small confidence. When Maldives was attacked by mercenaries, India chose to respond by sending in troops in consultation with other powers. Whether it was in respect of South Asia or China, India moved to defend its equities in national security. A diplomatic campaign was also waged to limit the presence of extra-regional navies in the Indian Ocean. The overall picture emerges of a growing regional power protective of its interests, but also more hopeful about creating a responsive neighbourhood.

This is not to suggest that things went India's way all through this period. The assassination of Sheikh Mujib in Dhaka in August 1975 significantly neutralized the gains of 1971. The politics of the Cold War also combined with Pakistan's mobilization of the Islamic world to block India at the Security Council elections of 1975. The Chinese attack on Vietnam in 1979 temporarily halted the correction in India's policy and perhaps undermined a serious overture in the making. The Soviet occupation of Afghanistan was even more complicating because it unleashed a new round of American military support for Pakistan. Indeed, this round was particularly devastating because it tapped into a larger Islamic fundamentalist resurgence. Sino-Pakistani collaboration that had receded when China was preoccupied with the Cultural Revolution also came back into play. Its three key elements were the physical link-up between the two countries through the Karakoram Highway in 1979, the intense nuclear and missile collaboration, and the coordination in respect to operations in Afghanistan. All of them have consequences to the present day for India.

Almost as significant was China's decision to change its position on the boundary negotiations in respect of the eastern sector. The renewed enmity of Pakistan combined with the hostility of the West on the Afghan issue also provided fertile ground for the external growth of the Khalistan movement. In terms of its sources of support, India was stuck with the Soviet presence in Afghanistan, which was a no-win situation in all circumstances. As the USSR came under pressure at the same time as India, the two countries became bound to each other even closer. For India, what started as an effective exploitation of a global contradiction ended as an impasse of some consequence.

The 1980s perhaps offers even more insights than the 1960s, mainly as it saw transformational events. Three of them merit special attention: Afghanistan as a reading of global politics, Sri Lanka as the challenge of boots on the ground, and China as the benefit of playing contradictions. The most consequential, without doubt, was the Afghan jihad. Looking back, it appears that India misjudged the extent to which Western countries would utilize it to damage the USSR. More relevant, the intensity of their support created the window for Pakistan to go through with its nuclear programme. It could be argued that India had little choice in the matter even if it had read the situation better. But it did take a full generation to put behind us the consequences of these events. Today, some vicarious satisfaction can be derived from the fact that the first jihad has come back to haunt Western countries. But the strategic damage of this period is difficult to overstate. As for its catastrophic impact on the USSR, this was truly a black swan, one not foreseen even by the most experienced analysts of that era.

The second issue which has got less attention than it deserves was the peacekeeping intervention in Sri Lanka. The US had gone through a similar experience in Lebanon just a few years earlier. The question relates to the deployment of boots on the ground abroad. Fingers can be pointed in many directions, including limited comprehension of local attitudes and interests, lack of preparation, paucity of intelligence and counter-insurgency tactics. Interestingly, in the same period, Indian forces displayed great grit and determination in fighting off secessionist forces in Punjab and Jammu and Kashmir. As these memories recede and calls for deployment abroad recur from time to time, it is imperative that India carefully weighs the compulsions with its costs.

China's rise is especially instructive for India. It was driving diplomatically in the late 1970s efforts to forge a united front against the USSR. This is in contrast to its reluctance to intervene, even indirectly, in the 1971 Bangladesh conflict despite being exhorted to do so by the Nixon Administration. What changed during this period was a determination to break up the cooperative strand in the ties between the US and USSR that was constricting China's strategic space. So it utilized both the Vietnam and Afghanistan conflicts to that end. And thus created a favourable political climate for the flow of Western investments. So much so, that even when the Tiananmen incident happened, there were enough advocates abroad to mitigate the damage. Having more than achieved its strategic objectives when the USSR broke up, China altered course and made up with a Russia coming under pressure. For an Indian assessing this period, it is telling that a competitor willing to take greater risks and pursue strategic clarity not only got a decade's head start in economic growth but also a more favourable geopolitical balance. So much again for consistency.

Although the 1960s were termed the dangerous decade because of political uncertainty and national fragility, the term could as well be applied to the 1990s. The 1991 balance of payments crisis only brought to head what was an accumulation of policy outcomes of the previous generation. A quarter century later, the literature on the happenings largely focus on the domestic challenges. The foreign policy situation, however, was no less traumatic, and it took considerable ingenuity and courage to chart a path of recovery. The dissolution of the USSR had undercut a fundamental premise on which Indian foreign policy operated since 1971, perhaps even since 1955. Even worse, the Russia that followed immediately was focused almost exclusively on the West and briefly downgraded its ties with India. In such a situation, the Indian response was very mature. Maintaining the importance of Russia, it engaged the US much more intensively while also reaching out to China. That the Indian economy also opened out during this period was clearly helpful for these relationships.

In this period of flux, the ASEAN played a very critical role in facilitating India's interactions with Asian economies and serving as a new focal point for a foreign policy whose moorings had become shaky. The importance of the growing partnership with ASEAN and India's membership of the ASEAN Regional Forum had long-term implications that could not have been foreseen then. It not only changed Indian thinking but also opened a pathway for the cultivation of Japan and South Korea. In many ways, this period of adjustment laid the foundation for an India that could operate on multiple axis in international affairs with greater comfort.

This phase may have unfolded as India sought a way out of a difficult predicament when the postulates of its foreign policy were called into question. But it developed in due course into a larger defence of its strategic autonomy. Interestingly, it was when the polity was under real stress that its redlines acquired clarity, even internally. The first pressure point was on the nuclear weapon option and the initial challenge was to continue developing it without an open confrontation. The manner in which the Comprehensive Test Ban Treaty was framed finally left India with no choice but to eventually exercise its weapon option.

Similar challenges in safeguarding economic and developmental interests in the face of Western demands were evident in the negotiations on the TRIPS and the Kyoto Protocol. A domestic issue that added to India's vulnerability at this very juncture was the worsening situation in Jammu and Kashmir. Attempts to internationalize that and a threatened shift in the longstanding US position caused considerable concern. It is to the credit of that generation of leadership that a difficult predicament was resolved with considerable finesse. In some cases, long-pending course corrections such as upgrading relations with Israel helped. Through a combination of adjustments and initiatives, India's positioning at the end of the decade improved visibly, as indeed did its economy. The nuclear tests of 1998 and the declaration of weaponization stands out as a landmark, since this not only decisively resolved a persistent dilemma but also provided the attributes later on of a leading power.

The delay in doing so did permit Pakistan to equalize, but that country's political and economic shortcomings diminished the value of that step. A year later, the Kargil conflict provided an opportunity to address the Pakistani challenge again and do so with a demonstrated sense of responsibility. In the same period, the spread of the internet economy created a new bonding with the US and established India firmly in global circles as a tech power. The promise of Russia's revival with the accession of President Putin concluded the century on a promising note for India.

The international context at the beginning of the twenty-first century was, at first, one of continued unipolarity, even if signs of trouble began to surface. American technology dominance overshadowed the steady growth of emerging economies. It was perhaps this that led the US to underestimate China's potential for rapid economic growth and amazing exploitation of trade opportunities. The conflict in Yugoslavia provided an opportunity to once again stamp the authority of Western powers, oblivious to the long-term threats that would hit them soon. It was not surprising that during this period, India-US relations developed well and sought to put behind issues that constrained their growth.

The Kargil experience enhanced confidence levels between them and the awkwardly titled 'Next Steps in Strategic Partnership (NSSP)' followed thereafter in 2004 to address export-control restrictions more positively. In the aftermath of the 2005 Indo-US nuclear deal, this appears less bold than it was at the time. But it provided a vital step towards attempting a larger breakthrough on the nuclear issue. In-between, there was a sea change in the global setting with the September 11 attacks and an American return to Afghanistan. India's handling of this opportunity was skilful, and it positioned itself as a sympathetic but understanding partner willing to work to American comfort levels. In the US itself, the Indian community grew steadily as a result of the H-1B programme and acquired the ability to make its interest felt in US politics. Terrorism and tech were the two drivers of the transformation of Indo-US relations that, in turn, opened up new vistas for India. In both cases, the Indian government's adeptness at seizing the opportunity is as important to recognize as the significance of the events themselves.

Even as India embarked on ground-breaking initiatives with the US, it sought to balance that with progress on other important accounts. The initiation of the Russia-India-China grouping (RIC) in 2001 that was to provide the nucleus for BRICS was one such step. The invention of the Special Representatives mechanism on boundary negotiations with China in 2003 was another. This was taken forward with the 2005 Agreement on Political Parameters and Guiding Principles on the boundary issue that promised a forward movement. There was briefly even serious talk of a free trade agreement with China. Relations with France, which showed more understanding of India's nuclear tests than other P-5 states, intensified rapidly in the triad of defence, nuclear and space. Each of these trends was to continue for the next decade and a half as India strove to shape global outcomes by shifting its weight in various directions on different issues. That worked so long as there was a stable balance based on the pre-eminence of the US with other major powers offsetting its influence. But as American dominance reduced and the power of China rose sharply, the changing landscape made the old calculation increasingly difficult to practice.

In the period when India was balancing a dynamic situation, a development that merits special mention is the 2005 Indo-US nuclear deal. It does so because this agreement removed key impediments to the development of those ties and enabled them to reach the stage they have today. In addition, it helped shape the global perception of India and has surely contributed to the higher stature it now enjoys. In its essence, the deal sought to put aside prohibitions on nuclear cooperation that had a ripple impact on defence, on dual-use technology, and on space cooperation. By making an exception, it changed sentiment in India about the US very substantially.

From the American side, there was little doubt that the growing relevance of Asia was a key factor in driving a stronger relationship with a democratic and market-oriented India. Debates within our country on this issue are well known and centred around a political suspicion of the US, implications for the nuclear weapon programme and pressures on the relationship with Iran. Despite the radical nature of the initiative and the extremely complicated negotiations that arose due to the cooperation being predicated on legislation, India was able to ensure a successful outcome. It also paved the way for an exception to be made by the Nuclear Suppliers Group that contributed to negating the perception of India as an outlier in an important area. This visible spike in a relationship with the premier power naturally put pressure for growth in other ties. It produced immediate gains because key European powers and Russia were supportive for their own reasons. At that time, China's relations with both India and the US were sufficiently cooperative as to support an NSG waiver decision. A few years later, changed global equations produced very different results.

If the nuclear deal underlined the gains of balancing, its aftermath revealed the challenges of that exercise. Balancing requires all major relationships to remain positively in play so that one can be used to make gains in the other. The moment they flatten out, they become a constraint on each other. In 2005, the climate for the nuclear deal was built up carefully through an ambitious Defence Framework, an Open Skies agreement and strong business sentiment. After the nuclear deal, the handling of the civil nuclear liability issue, excessive defence expectations and frictions on the trade side between them dissipated the air of optimism. Combined with the Obama Administration's approach to the Af-Pak theatre and the controversy caused by the unjustified arrest of an Indian diplomat, ties were now dominated by irritants. Arriving in the US in December 2013 to take up the responsibility of an Ambassador, I found myself engaged more in damage control than in consolidating a breakthrough. It took a change of government in New Delhi to create a change of mood. But the lesson really is one of the importance of tending to ties. On both sides.

It was not only the dampening of sentiment with the US that made balancing a difficult exercise by 2014. A very serious structural shift had taken place with the global financial crisis of

2008-09. While the election of Barack Obama created a sense of hope, the retrenchment of American power began with the withdrawal from Iraq and the promise to do so in Afghanistan. With the passage of time, it was evident that the US no longer had the inclination to meet global challenges as in the past. Nowhere was that more evident than in the Asia-Pacific.At the same time, as Ambassador in Beijing after 2009, I was witness first-hand to the growing sense of confidence in the Chinese establishment about its own pace of rise. The change of guard in China heralded a different era, as much for that nation as for its relations with the world. During this very period, India's own ties with China became more complex. Controversies over stapled visas, military contacts and border intrusions all portended a new phase. This was also a time when China's presence in India's immediate periphery acquired greater visibility. While speculation about a possible G-2 between the US and China remained, the reality was that the US now had less to offer and China a greater ask. As events unfolded, political changes in India also brought new factors in play.

By 2014, the global situation compelled India to conceptualize its foreign policy goals in a different way. It first had to recognize the greater multipolarity and uncertainty that characterized international affairs. Nations were combining on narrower issues rather than broad approaches. To a large extent, world affairs now looked like a global marketplace with less pre-conceptions and more transactions.

In this background, India set out to deliberately raise its global profile, consciously influence international gatherings and negotiations, purposefully increase high-level contacts and ambitiously invest in building linkages and connectivity. The primary objective was to consolidate its position in Asia. But, in parallel, India also made an effort to think beyond. Within

Asia, obviously, the neighbourhood came first and the very act of inviting their leaders together in 2014 at the time of swearing in sent a clear message of change. In South Asia, India now became a votary of positive regionalism and expressed that through expanded commitments to connectivity and development projects. It did take into account the identity politics so deeply rooted in its periphery but calculated that structural linkages can compensate in the longer run. Given that most of these nations are democratic, the pressures of electoral cycles and competitive politics also had to be managed.

Predictably, Pakistan has posed a particular challenge in view of its continuing practice of cross-border terrorism. Combined with its resistance to connectivity, it is clearly not on the same page as the other states of South Asia. A more confident India has demonstrated boldness both ways: in a willingness to engage as underlined by a dramatic prime ministerial visit to Lahore, as well as in a determination to conduct cross-LOC and cross-boundary strikes when required. Afghanistan has also been brought much closer, politically and psychologically. The implementation of the Chabahar port project and the provision of security assistance to the Afghan military reflects this fresh approach.

In keeping with its growing interests and aspirations, there is also now a stronger feel for the extended neighbourhood. Where South-East Asia is concerned, the earlier Look East policy has been given greater teeth through stronger project implementation focus and turned into Act East. This has been dovetailed into a more determined development of its own North-East states and coordinated with greater access and connectivity in Bangladesh. Relations with South-East Asia have acquired a greater security dimension and higher stronger political profile, underlined by the presence of all ASEAN leaders at the Republic Day celebrations in 2018. On the other side, the relatively narrow relations with Gulf countries, earlier focused mainly on energy and community, have also acquired similar facets of security and politics. It did require greater dexterity, given the divisions among Gulf countries and their issues with Iran.

The same sense of purpose has guided an integrated approach to the maritime domain, spelt out by the SAGAR doctrine in March 2015, that has created a basis for robust cooperation with Indian Ocean island nations and beyond.

In recent years, India has concluded White Shipping agreements with seventeen nations, provided coastal surveillance radars to eight of them, naval capabilities to six, and set up an integrated fusion centre for maritime domain awareness. It has extended soft Lines of Credit in the field of defence to eleven nations, deputed training teams to eleven as well, and offered capacity building to a large number of foreign militaries. Its hydrographic cooperation covers five countries in the Indian Ocean. And its three annual HADR exercises have helped it to mount seven major operations in the last five years, stretching from Fiji to Yemen and Mozambique. The reality is that in maritime policy too, India could succeed in doing more with less. A lighter footprint, applications of technology, embrace of partnerships and a propensity towards frugality have come together. The net impact of all this has been very much more because working with international partners has provided a multiplier effect.

Africa has also started to be treated as the neighbourhood beyond the horizon. The India-Africa Forum Summit in October 2015 saw the unprecedented participation of all fifty-four nations, forty-one of them at the leader level. Visits of the senior Indian leadership to Africa have been stepped up sharply and the development assistance and training put on a firmer track. The decision to open new embassies in eighteen African nations speaks of the priority that this region is now receiving. A greater outreach to Latin America, the Caribbean, Pacific Islands and Oceania is also now distinctly visible. How much India can exploit the opportunities that await depends to a great degree on this broader engagement.

Like other major powers, India too has turned to development partnerships as a significant instrument in its diplomatic tool kit. And it has done so in its own unique India Way. Overall, it has offered 300 Lines of Credit to sixty-four countries involving 540 projects. The bulk of the LoCs and projects are with Africa, now at 321 projects involving 205 LoCs. In addition, India currently has 181 projects in Asia, thirty-two in Latin America and Caribbean and three each in Central Asia and Oceania. These initiatives have qualitatively expanded in recent years, especially in terms of the size of the LoCs and the complexity of the projects. Their planning and execution has also become more efficient by a more integrated approach and stronger oversight. The dispersal of grant assistance is even broader than the Lines of Credit, covering virtually all developing regions of the world. Africa has been a particular focus of attention, partly as a reflection of our solidarity born out of shared struggles. But it is also an aspect of strategy, as the rise of Africa will add to the multipolarity of the world. As others have discovered before, such development partnerships provide the foundation for long-lasting relationships.

Prominent Indian-supported projects cover the power sector in Sudan, Rwanda, Zimbabwe and Malawi; water in Mozambique, Tanzania and Guinea; health in Cote d'Ivoire, Guinea and Zambia; sugar plants in Ethiopia and Ghana; cement in Djibouti and Republic of Congo; and government buildings in the Gambia and Burundi. In fact, in several African countries, some of the manufacturing plants we have set up are truly the first of their kind. This steady growth in Indian interests in Africa is reflected in an expanded footprint and a deeper engagement: 51 out of 54 nations of that continent host such development projects, while the training collaboration covers 10,000 Africans annually. Two digital initiatives are also on a pilot mode in Africa today – the e-Vidya Bharati distance education and the e-Aarogya Bharati distance health. More than the cooperation itself, this aspect of India's foreign policy underlines its progressive emergence on the global stage.

The lessons of the past can be captured in five baskets of issues. The first relates to the need for greater realism in policy. Particularly in the phase of optimistic non-alignment, maybe even later, our focus on diplomatic visibility sometimes led to overlooking the harsher realities of hard security. The early misreading of Pakistan's intentions can perhaps be explained away by lack of experience. But the reluctance to attach overriding priority to securing borders even a decade later is much more difficult to justify. It was not that the challenges of 1962 were unanticipated. It was more that a diplomacy focused on world politics did not give it the primacy it deserved. Somewhere, there was an implicit but entrenched belief that India's high standing in world affairs was protection enough against global turbulence and competitive politics. It was, therefore, at some cost that we discovered that outcomes can be decided as much on the field as at conferences. This is a relevant takeaway even now, despite having entered a more constrained world.

Interestingly, India did not shrink from the applications of force when required. Hyderabad in 1948 and Goa in 1961 are illustrative examples, as indeed is Kashmir when attacked by Pakistan. But having so strongly built up an image of a reluctant power, we also ended up influenced by our own narrative.

Due to that, we also rarely prepared for security situations with the sense of mission that many of our competitors displayed.

Discomfort with hard power was reflected in lack of adequate consultation with the military, most notably during the 1962 conflict. The creation of a Chief of Defence Staff half a century later shows how far we have travelled. Judgments of the past that overlooked security implications are also worth studying. An overemphasis on diplomacy also led to a lack of understanding of the behaviour of other polities. The Cold War was seen more as an argumentation, when the reality was a ruthless exercise of power. There was also little awareness in the 1950s that we were dealing with a battle-hardened neighbour to the North. Or of the strategic significance of Pakistan-occupied Kashmir.

This approach to world affairs continued even thereafter. Thus, in 1972 at Shimla, India chose to bet on an optimistic outlook on Pakistan. However, it resulted in both a revanchist Pakistan and a continuing problem in Jammu and Kashmir. That it has taken us so long to link talks with Pakistan to cessation of terrorism speaks for itself. Without overstating the argument, a case can certainly be made for a more grounded Indian approach to international relations.

The economic counterpart of these concerns constitutes a second basket. If one considers all the major growth stories after 1945, a common feature was the extraordinary focus that they put on leveraging the global environment for national development. China did that with great effect, initially with the USSR and then with the US and the West. The Asian 'tiger economies' practised it as well, using Japan, the US and now China successively to build themselves. That is how India too approached its various relationships over the last seven decades, but not always with the same single-mindedness. Nevertheless, much of India's industrialization and capacities in other domains were direct achievements of collaborations enabled by diplomacy. Steel, nuclear industry, higher education and computing are some examples. This held true even more for the post-1991 reform period and the shift eastwards of India's economic centre of gravity.

The interconnection between diplomacy, strategy and economic capabilities is, however, not always self-evident. As in security, it is important to distinguish between cause and effect. The economy drives diplomacy; not the other way around. Few would argue that the reforms of the 1990s and greater openness have served us well for some years. But as we then extrapolated it onto free trade agreements with South-East and East Asia, the proposition became more challengeable. Blame it on structural rigidities, limited competitiveness, inadequate exploitation of opportunities or just unfair practices: the growing deficit numbers are a stark reality. More importantly, their negative impact on industry at home is impossible to deny. And China, of course, poses a special trade challenge even without an FTA.

Any quest to maximize options and expand space naturally requires engaging multiple players. Conceptually, this third basket is a given in Indian foreign policy since there is a basic consensus about nurturing our independence. While doing well in the first decade of a bipolar world, we also discovered the associated danger of being left short on all accounts. As India saw in 1962, the best of both worlds is easier imagined than realized. In the periods thereafter, the distance from one pole was also not automatically compensated by the other. Sometimes, global circumstances require us – as in 1971 – to lean on one side, just as China itself did in 1950 and 1971. As a general rule, extracting more from the international system depends on the bigger picture and a zero-sum game cannot be an assumption. Indeed, a particularly disturbing scenario that nations like India and China faced in the 1960s was the prospect of the superpowers finding common ground. That is why the talk of a G-2 even decades later created such deep unease again in so many quarters. Hedging is a delicate exercise, whether it is the non-alignment and strategic autonomy of earlier periods, or multiple engagements of the future. But there is no getting away from it in a multipolar world. This is a game best played on the front foot, appreciating that progress on any one front strengthens that on all others.

To the uninitiated or the anachronistic, the pursuit of apparently contradictory approaches may seem baffling. How does one reconcile a Howdy Modi gathering with a Mamallapuram or a Vladivostok Summit? Or the RIC (Russia-India-China) with JAI (Japan-America-India)? Or the Quad and the SCO (Shanghai Cooperation Organization)? An Iran with the Saudis, or Israel with Palestine? The answer is in a willingness to look beyond dogma and enter the real world of convergences. Think of it as calculus, not just as arithmetic. This new version of world affairs is a challenge for practitioners and analysts alike, but one that must be mastered to forge ahead.

Risk-taking is an inherent aspect of diplomacy and most policy judgments revolve around its mechanics. It is also a natural accompaniment to hedging. When we look at this fourth basket, it is evident that a low-risk foreign policy is only likely to produce limited rewards. On occasions when India departed from this mode, some risks paid off while others did not. We laid out our broad approach as early as 1946 and developed that framework as time went on. Although India came under pressure in 1962 and 1971, it limited the compromises that it had to make and sought to revert to the earlier posture as and when it could. Over the course of its rise, it introduced new concepts and terms to deal with emerging issues, without necessarily abandoning the earlier ones. The cumulative impression was thus of a steady and middle-of-the-road approach that gathered greater substance as India's influence grew. Having noted that, the truth is that ascending up the global ladder did require taking big calls, whether conventional or nuclear, political or economic. Not all risks are necessarily dramatic; many just require the confident calculations and determined follow through of day-to-day policy management. Their aggregate impact can result in a quantum jump in global positioning. To a certain degree, we see that happening today.

The fifth basket is in a return to the primer: reading the global tea leaves right. The foreign policy of all nations is set against the backdrop of global contradictions. They reflect an assessment of opportunities and compulsions, risks and rewards. Even if we are to get our immediate situation right, a misreading of the larger landscape can prove to be costly. In our own case, going to the UN on Jammu and Kashmir clearly misread the intent of the Anglo-American alliance and the seriousness of the Cold War. Years later, our early awareness about growing Sino-Soviet differences did not mature on our expected timelines. In the 1960s, 1980s and again after 2001, we underestimated the relevance of Pakistan to American and Chinese global strategy.

This is not to suggest that India has not had its successes. Indo-Soviet and later Indo-Russian relations are a direct product of our global strategizing. After 1991, so too has been the adjustment in our policy towards the US. Both the Indo-Soviet Treaty and the India-US Nuclear Deal were outcomes of a larger reading of world affairs. That is the case with correctives introduced in respect of the US in 1973 and China in 1976 to overcome the 1971 polarization with both. Identifying the opportunities thrown up by the structure of world politics can also help mitigate risks. We saw that, for example, in respect to France after the 1998 nuclear tests. Today, an appreciation of world politics must include a proper understanding of Sino-US contradictions, of growing multipolarity, of weaker multilateralism, of larger economic and political rebalancing, of greater space for regional powers, and of the world of convergences. Each of them is a factor in driving the policy initiatives of the present era. Whether it is our outreach to the Gulf, the advocacy of Indo-Pacific or more vigorous engagement of Europe, they represent a facet of a larger repositioning.

So what are the prospects of the sixth phase that is now underway? A changing world is clearly a more actionable one for those who do not wish to get left behind. For a beginning, it requires a thinking that keeps up with times. A clearer definition of interests is the next step and its determined pursuit the one thereafter. We see that today, for example, in a better appreciation of our maritime geography and the SAGAR doctrine. When confronted by security challenges, this India has also responded with a new grit. Its enthusiasm for shaping global conversations on climate change, terrorism, connectivity and maritime security is already having an impact. The relief operations undertaken in Yemen, Nepal, Iraq, Sri Lanka, Maldives, Fiji and Mozambique are statements of capability as much as responsibility. Its election-winning record in international organizations is another important statement. Expanded offers of development assistance have been accompanied by an improved record of project execution. The neighbourhood and Africa will testify to this change. India's branding has become much stronger, including through the International Day of Yoga, the International Solar Alliance or, most recently, the Coalition for Disaster Resilient Infrastructure.

While the previous phases of foreign policy each have a neat description, it is harder to categorize the current one. Part of the challenge is that we are still in the early phase of a major transition. The contours of the near future are not yet clear. One solution is to anchor it on Indian aspirations and to speak of our goal of emerging as a leading power. The problem is that others tend to take it as a statement of arrival rather than a goal on the horizon. Taking off on non-alignment, it is sometimes useful to speak of multi-alignment. It appears more energetic and participative as compared to an earlier posture of abstention or non-involvement. The difficulty is that it also appears opportunistic, whereas India is really seeking strategic convergence rather than tactical convenience. Putting India First may be another way of capturing a strong and pragmatic policy outlook. This suffers from a comparison with other nations who have chosen to be more self-centred. In India's case, nationalism has in fact led to greater internationalism. Advancing prosperity and influence may be a fair description but is not exactly a catch word. Perhaps we need to accept that a single phrase may elude us for some time in the midst of global uncertainty.

As India stands poised to move to the next level, did we lose valuable time in doing so? Such queries are often a product of hindsight and may lack context. Nevertheless, these are issues that could be pondered about, especially if we speak of outcomes of judgment rather than of circumstances. Our ties with China are a natural beginning for such a discussion. Should India, for example, have brought the boundary issue to a head in 1950 itself? Could the border conflict of 1962 have been avoided by a compromise in 1960 when Zhou Enlai came to India? With the US, did our cultural antipathy in the initial years aggravate the sense of distance? On economic issues, there is probably more consensus that India should have followed the example of ASEAN and China and opened up a decade before it actually did. On the strategic side, the delay in its self-declaration as a nuclear weapon power from 1974 to 1998 may well have been the worst of all worlds. Were we prisoners to paper, a trait that came close to wrecking the 2005 nuclear deal as well? Our handling of Pakistan, a society which we are supposed to know well, also raises many questions.

These are not exactly theoretical situations and are cited to underline the contention that emergence as a leading power requires great pragmatism. That can be further strengthened by more sophisticated narratives that help reconcile divergences. After all, our emphasis on sovereignty has not prevented us from responding to human rights situations in our immediate region. Nor have the steps that India has taken to ensure its integrity and promote regional security – whether in Hyderabad, Goa, Sri Lanka or Maldives – made us less multilateral.

Entrenched views are naturally strongest on the more perennial challenges. In the case of India, this relates most of all to Pakistan. Changes in thinking will trigger a debate and that has been the case for the past few years. That fact is that we had allowed the narrative to focus mainly on a dialogue, when the real issue had become stopping cross-border terrorism. Dogma treats every new approach as an unjustified deviation. In the last five years, however, a different normal has developed and global conversations on cross-border terrorism have become more serious. Just look at the FATF as proof of this assertion. As we move decisively to combat separatism in Jammu and Kashmir, there is some talk of its internationalization and hyphenation of our ties with Pakistan. This is thinking from the past, reflecting neither the strength of India, the mood of the nation or the determination of the government. Uninformed comments abroad on our internal affairs is hardly internationalization. And the reputational and real differences between India and Pakistan puts paid to any hyphenation effort. In reality, these fears are but a thinly disguised advocacy of inaction. Their intent, conscious or otherwise, is to legitimize a status quo that has now been overtaken by history.

The balance sheet for India's foreign policy after seven decades presents a mixed picture. National development is at the heart of any assessment, and it is difficult to quarrel with the view that there has been significant progress, but not enough. The comparison with what China achieved in the same period is sobering. Reading the big picture right and then operating in the international situation could have gone better. Instead, the mantra of unchanging foreign policy axioms has discouraged an honest review of our performance and the introduction of timely correctives. Diligence and debate have not been as rigorous as they should for an aspiring player. When combined with the hesitations of history, it has led to unexplored avenues and unrealized outcomes.

We are now at the cusp of change. With more confidence, the pursuit of seemingly divergent goals and the straddling of contradictions are being attempted. Taking risks is inherent to the realization of ambitions. A nation that has the aspiration to become a leading power some day cannot continue with unsettled borders, an unintegrated region and under-exploited opportunities. Above all, it cannot be dogmatic in approaching a changing global order. The world that awaits us not only calls for fresh thinking, but eventually, a new consensus as well. Putting dogmas behind us is a starting point for that journey.

5

Of Mandarins and Masses

Public Opinion and the West

'Mother India is in many ways the mother of us all'

— WILL DURANT

It may be hard for diplomats to digest, but the Indian Street has often displayed better instincts than Lutyens' Delhi when it comes to assessing opportunities and risks abroad. Their geopolitical understanding may not be formal. But they intuitively know with whom to trade and where to travel. Their choices in emigration and education were made well ahead of policy shifts by Indian diplomacy. A game-changing event like 9/11 was seen for what it was. The sharp popular imagery of nations has also captured the complexity of diplomacy. Say what you will, but the Street has a well-developed instinct, whether it is about Russia or America, China or Pakistan.

Now, this is not to suggest that the measured deliberations of statecraft are less important than the passions of society. But it is also a fact that we have entered a different era where the availability of information, tools of technology and cultural identities drive contemporary nationalism. The democratization of societies that bring to the fore more grounded politics also contributes to this process. Therefore, convolutions of policy and the accumulated weight of experiences sometimes struggle to meet the demands of society, particularly on issues where public opinion is exercised. The challenge today is to strike the right balance between societal dynamics and the mechanics of policymaking. Mandarins can no longer be impervious to the masses.

An inability to reconcile the two can only come at the cost of political credibility, a phenomenon that we have seen in so many other countries. India is obviously not immune to this paradigm shift and the changed discourse reflects a newer era with its own driving forces. How to capture Indian nationalism in policy terms is a complex task that must simultaneously address issues of history, identity, interests and politics. The welfare of the diaspora is not irrelevant to this matrix. Relating all of that to the West and the old order, as indeed to the rise of China, is an associated question.

Among the more arrogant assertions of an era of hubris was that of the 'end of history'. The complacency of this pronouncement is only matched by its limitation as a Eurocentric analysis that disregarded what was happening in Asia at the same time. But nevertheless, we were supposedly staring at a universal and invincible globalized order led by the US. However, what appeared then as permanent was a transient moment of American unipolarity, as it was with other powers in history before. Larger competitiveness and political contestation proceeded to return the world to a more natural diversity. In the process, it was discovered that like fashions, the world of politics also has its cycles. After decades of globalization being touted as politically correct and economically inevitable, we are seeing a dramatic revival of nationalism across geographies. Some have been more subtle and gradual; others unexpected and impactful. They are each different and specific to their society, yet part of a larger statement of cultural beliefs.

When Donald Trump rejected globalism in favour of patriotism at the UN in September 2018, he may have typically overstated his case. But the underlying reality is hard to wish away. As electoral outcomes have affirmed across continents, the trend line today points towards stronger cultural identities and more nationalist narratives. Whether it is in aspiration or in anxiety, we are witnessing a return to history rather than an end to it. In cases like China, it is an outcome of newly developed capabilities. But we also see nations like Russia, Turkey or Iran exercise influence without there being an objective difference in their circumstances. Nationalism appears to be the X-factor in such situations. These global trends are reflected in domestic debates where cosmopolitanism is held responsible for the loss of livelihood as much as of identity. And indeed, how nationalism as a concept is perceived tells us much about a society.

Broadly, the West has been less comfortable with it than Asia, where it is regarded as a natural corollary of economic progress. This, of course, has now started to change with the coming of Trump. But there are specific histories at work that explain why Germany and Japan shy away while a Russia or Turkey may flaunt it. China has come to the game late, having used it as a diplomatic tool for long. But for much of the developing world, especially nations that have regained independence from colonial rule, nationalism is synonymous with asserting independence. Whether optimistic or not, polities in different predicaments are now going down that path – witness the China Dream, Brexit or America First. The linkage between globalization, regime credibility and a return to history is unmistakable.

The real truth about this revival of nationalism is that it has actually been a very durable basis for organizing societies. At various times, it has defeated conflicting ideologies that appealed to both larger and narrower loyalties. Multinational empires struggled with nationalist sentiment and by and large, lost out. But national entities that encountered sub-national dissensions have usually won. Western imperialism was eventually undone by nationalist sentiments awakening in their former colonies. Communism was the next of the transnational ideologies on a global scale. This too eventually foundered when socialism acquired national characteristics. The schism between the USSR and China, and later between China and Vietnam, affirmed the enduring appeal of nationalism.

Faith-based movements have also attempted to cut across national divides. These may use causes like that of Palestine or be an effort for a specific purpose like Bosnia or Afghanistan. The rise of the Daesh-Islamic State is a refinement of this model. Being outcomes of high emotion and exceptional circumstances, nationalism eventually returns them to business as usual.

The globalization of our era represents yet another effort at transcending an entrenched organizational principle of modern politics. But because it rests on a deeper technology basis and stronger economic interests, its tension with nationalism will continue for the foreseeable future. Contestation between two such powerful rationalizations is not unnatural. So, rather than visualize either of them as an event, we should see them as currents of history.

Coming in different sizes and shapes, nationalism can be assertive, reactive or just expressive. The confident category reflects the real and psychological outcome of shifts in the world power hierarchy. It is represented by the rise of nations like China and India, of a continent like Asia and the consequent rebalancing of the global order. This is evident in both the content and tenor of international conversations. It is visible also in most major conferences and negotiations. In fact, the very perception of who are key world leaders and the newer formats for their gathering – such as G-20 or BRICS – underline this evolution. Not just that, the global agenda itself is undergoing a change, reflecting more diverse interests than before. The outcomes of key negotiations, such as the Paris climate change accord, also reflect this changed reality. So too do the creation of new institutions like the Asian Infrastructure Investment Bank or the International Solar Alliance. The demand for fairer representation in bodies like the IMF and the continued pressure for UN reform are other such manifestations. China is the great disrupter here since unlike Japan, South Korea or the ASEAN, its emergence cannot be accommodated in the old framework. The rise of India will only reinforce this pressure for change. For all their other differences, the demand for a more contemporary global order does put India and China on the same side of the table.

A second driver of greater nationalism is its very opposite: the reaction in more privileged societies to this rebalancing. The offshoring of manufacturing and creation of extensive global supply chains has inevitably had an impact on the West. The consequent resentment has been aggravated by a perception that some have taken unfair advantage of the global trading system. As immigrant flows expand, they too contribute to a sense of loss of power in certain income groups. Ironically, the immediate crisis in Europe was sparked less by these happenings and more by refugees from conflict situations for which the West itself has responsibility. Be that as it may, the outcome has still been a hybrid economic-cultural protectionism which has found traction in political opinion.

A third category is the accumulated impact of how sharper cultural identities across the world have played on each other. The epicentre for that has been West Asia; and other regions have reacted to it over time. While the cause and effect of this process can always be debated, the fact is that there is a change in how people define themselves and perceive others. As a result, many of the broader identity constructs have come under challenge. As these trends fuse, the balance between economics, politics, culture, faith and identity has been disturbed. This will obviously vary from country to country and have its own dynamics. We should expect uneasy coexistence and shifting equations between globalist and nationalist forces as neither can prevail. And the world it will produce will be very contentious.

India is no exception to the larger trends that have strengthened nationalism. Ordinary people have strong feelings on national welfare and collective prospects. They respond not just to surgical strikes like Uri and Balakot or a border face-off but even to more arcane issues like membership of the Nuclear Suppliers Group or elections to international bodies. The steady growth of its economy and the emergence of an aspirational generation with greater connectivity to the world fuels this process. There are social forces at work as well, as our power structure has broadened over the years to capture greater diversity and reflect stronger roots.

In emotional terms, nationalism obviously contributes to a stronger sense of unity. In political terms, it signifies a greater determination to combat both sub-national and supra-national challenges to it. In policy terms, it focuses on how to maximize national capabilities and influence. In India's current situation, that has a particular relevance to security. Overall, a nationalistic foreign policy outlook is likely to approach the world with more confidence and greater realism. What may be different about India is that unlike in many other powers, that sense of nationalism does not translate into an 'us versus the world' mentality. For reasons that derive from our innate pluralism, there is a tradition of reconciling the nationalism with global engagement. Not driven by victimhood, it has the potential to serve as a bridge between the established and emerging orders.

Nationalism being a product of politics and identity, India has had to grapple with both when it comes to its immediate periphery. Its civilizational influence has obviously been much broader than contemporary political boundaries. But new nationalisms may not be readily amenable to building on old connections. As a result, its interface with proximate areas as well as extended neighbours was significantly diluted. The challenge, therefore, is to rebuild a fractured region while re-establishing linkages beyond. The two goals can be self-supporting if both processes go well; or much harder if either stumble.

Where South Asia is concerned, shared history and divided sociology make for natural sensitivity. A resulting wariness is sometimes visible, especially in elite attitudes. That must be addressed as India builds understanding with society as a whole. It would require providing larger reassurance, while offering greater incentives for closer cooperation. A polity like India should display the wisdom of treating its prosperity as a lifting tide for the entire region. That means assigning a higher degree of attention and greater resources, a policy captured by Neighbourhood First.

Neighbours pose challenges everywhere and India cannot escape having its fair share. To keep such relationships steady, India should invest in greater structural inter-linkages. These could help mitigate situations that would inevitably arise from time to time. Having recognized that, it is also important that where there are real problems, we do not duck them. Generosity and firmness must go hand in hand. In the last few years, India has done well where it has defined its interests with clarity and trusted its own instincts. It has also been the magnet around which global opinion has crystallized in respect of the region. That it has responded positively to those neighbours who are prepared to engage India more intensively is also a welcome development.

At a time when most are pursuing interests narrowly, it is to India's benefit that it takes a more expansive view of the world. By stepping forward in difficult situations, it can not only underline its greater capabilities and confidence but also build its unique brand as a generous power. This imagery fits in well with the embrace of the world that is inherent in Indian thinking and reinforces its positioning as a power that can bridge divides.

The unfolding of this approach has been in the making over the last few years. It has been expressed especially through initiatives responding to natural calamities. These activities have helped to prepare the nation to be the first responder to crisis situations in the larger region. India has surely but steadily assisted in underwriting the global commons when that has come under stress. Its physical presence is supported by declared respect for international law and norms, a position which it has made credible by setting an example in dispute resolution. Nationalism, contributing to global good, is powerful for brand building.

Given history, it is natural that the rise of nationalism across regions should impact the Westernization of the world. Our world functions largely in the framework of Western concepts and norms. At least in Asia, we can talk of an economic rise with attendant cultural confidence. Other continents are nowhere close to this situation. Even in Asia, the picture is very mixed in respect of compromises and assertions. A comparison of India, China and Japan is interesting in bringing out where these societies have adapted, and where they have held on to their own. While they each offer enough evidence to portray their relationship with the West in easy or difficult terms, the decisive factor has always been the politics of the day.

At every stage of their modernization, these societies have calculated and recalculated their equation with the West. But as Asia makes its influence felt more in the global arena, their national expressions are difficult to keep in check. From limited political assertions, they are moving to broader societal and historical statements. How far these branding exercises will develop and what their impact will be on finding common ground globally is hard to predict.

In dealing with the West, the Chinese often invoke a century of humiliation to justify their positions now. But if anybody should be complaining, it should be India which saw two – not one – centuries of rape and pillaging by Europe. This despoiling of a leading economy of its times is still to be widely appreciated. A 2018 study estimated that the resources drained from India by the UK alone were as much as $ 45 trillion by current value.

The numbers serve to highlight a scale of the looting systematically underplayed by Western narratives. The evidence is there for all to observe, not least the assets with others that have a direct India provenance. Nevertheless, imperialism produced a history accepted in many quarters even today that British rule was somehow beneficial to Indians. The real record, of course, is of creating poverty, opium trade, slavery and famine on a mass scale. Remorse over this dark chapter of history is limited even now. Instead, glorification of this era remains the primary narrative as museums continue to proudly display artefacts that do not belong to them.

Yet, it is remarkable that despite growing consciousness of these depredations, Indians bear little grudge. What has really distinguished India from the China of the 1950-60s or the Japan of the 1930s was that it never resorted to domestic mobilization on the basis of anti-Western sentiment. This largely non-frictional but not always cordial record of ties between the West and India is noteworthy. Once India set history aside and let politics take over, convergences of values and interests between India and the West started to take shape. After all, there is much that they do share, including a liberal democratic political model, similar governance practices, a credible market economy and commitment to the rule of law. That India after Independence chose to continue its close ties with the English-speaking world was a politico-cultural decision of no small consequence. Over years thereafter, a very substantive relationship that covered politics, security, trade, investment, services, innovation, education and development assistance was built up, especially with the US and the UK. This was characterized by extensive contacts between civil societies and institutions. The large Indian diaspora in many Western societies strengthened the bonding.

At challenging moments in India's contemporary history, economic and military support from the West has made a critical difference. This was particularly the case in the 1960s, after the border conflict with China, and during years of famine. India was the largest recipient of development assistance from Western nations and the multilateral banks they controlled. As it embarked on reforms thirty years ago and shifted to higher growth rates, the West was again supportive of this trajectory. They have also advanced India's political interests thereafter in the international system, including through the Indo-US nuclear deal and its membership of various export control regimes. On the major international issues of the day, such as terrorism, maritime security or connectivity, there is now a considerable meeting of minds. This relationship has increasingly made itself felt in global affairs, especially after 9/11.

The European Union, the UK and the US are among the top economic partners and sources of capital, technology and best practices that are necessary for India's modernization. The maturing of ties is also reflected in two-way flows, with Indian companies now emerging as significant foreign investors in Western economies. The politics of these ties has kept pace. While the India-US relationship, in particular, has flowered in recent years, the 'third option' that Europe has long represented on strategic issues has grown in importance. These accumulated developments have today created high degree of comfort between India and the West.

While appreciating where we have reached today, it must also be acknowledged that this was not always the state of our ties. An honest account would start from the partition of the Subcontinent that diminished India's influence so much. An artificial twinning of India with Pakistan was deliberately created, one that was broken only in 1971. There was also for many years an interest in politically exploiting fissures within Indian society. The latitude extended even today to separatist activities citing democratic freedoms is troubling.

Western association in our neighbourhood till a few years ago was often with political forces that sought greater distance from India. If India's democratic values are currently extolled, this too was not always the case. On the contrary, military regimes in the Subcontinent were held out as examples of efficiency in the past. The broad approach was to keep India in play, and yet to also keep it in check. An unstable or weak India was as undesirable as a strong and domineering one. It was, in truth, a Goldilocks approach to the Indian porridge – not too hot, nor too cold, needing some effort to get it just right. And this was the India policy of most Western foreign offices. Therefore, we have the paradox of assisting India when it was really down after the 1962 conflict; yet of opposition when it asserts itself, as in the 1971 Bangladesh emergence. The phases in-between are of steady engagement but on a cautious scale. Indian aspirations of industrialization, building defence, nuclear or space capabilities or attaining positions of international influence were dealt with prudence, even while there was broad support for its development.

Much of this was rationalized by the argument that India, with its non-alignment policy, was not with the West in the Cold War.

Understandably, the Indian narrative is very different and Western partiality for Pakistan is attributed as a reason for driving it closer to the Soviet bloc. All of this has, however, substantially changed. And with it, really, India's relationship with Western nations as a whole and its key players in particular.

There are, however, still divisive issues that speak for continuum of policy on both sides. On a range of economic and social questions, Indian and Western interests are quite divergent. Many involve policies where the welfare of millions is at stake. India also speaks for a larger developing world constituency insofar as equity and fairness are concerned. This divergence is reflected in trade, climate change and intellectual property positions. As each party tries to frame issues and set priorities to its advantage, these contradictions will continue. India has a powerful constituency in the global South that it must cultivate even as it rises. It would be a more South-Western power than the West may desire.

In the world of security and politics, India sometimes suffers collateral damage of Western initiatives. A case to the point was the Afghanistan jihad in the 1980s that went on to fuel terrorism in Jammu and Kashmir. Developments in Afghanistan and West Asia remain of concern even today. Perceptions and priorities can also differ significantly if vantage points are not the same. On nuclear proliferation, the Western focus on Iran and North Korea stands out in contrast to the whitewashing of Pakistan and the fairy tale of a private A.Q. Khan network. On the question of civil liberties and human rights, a military regime to India's East – in Myanmar- was sanctioned at the very time when one to its West – in Pakistan – was hailed as an ally. When it came to the great tragedies of our era, whether it is the famine in China or mass killings in Bangladesh and Cambodia, strategic calculations of the West trumped public outrage. Old habits explain why the countries that contribute troops to UN peacekeeping have little say in the mandates. Or that the bombing of an Air India aircraft off Ireland is treated so differently from that of PanAm over Lockerbie four years later. We have seen societies that overlook advocacy of terrorism in the name of free speech then practise rendition when their own security is at stake.

There are lessons for both India and the West to draw from these examples. For all the changes in the world, India should not underestimate the influence that the West still retains. On its part, the West should appreciate that India is coming from a different place with a different history. There will inevitably be some divergences, even as the common ground expands.

The key to Western durability till now is the set of institutions and practices that it progressively but firmly established in the period of its dominance. There is virtually no sector of human activity that in some form or the other is not shaped or regulated by it. Rules are set for the entire world, as well as for the global commons. These are supported by narratives that serve the West well, while diminishing its competitors. The mix of institutions, regimes, regulations and understandings is such a complex web that creating alternatives is truly a formidable challenge. However, as global power redistribution progresses, this will inevitably happen.

If the entrenched have to compromise with the emerging, the issue is not of the extent and nature alone. More important, it is with whom all it should do so. With China, the Western logic of engagement has been primarily that of mutual economic gain. If there are stresses today, that is because its mutuality has come under some questioning. But India is a different case, because there is also a political overlay to the economic logic. Its pluralistic character and democratic outlook is closer to that of the West. India's economic growth and political stature, as a result, is today imbued with a larger significance. Contributing to its rise can be part of shaping the new global strategic balance. India too would do well to recall that in history, some nations have been partnered by others reflecting a larger calculus.

It is not just India's capabilities but also the relative weight of the West that is changing. If the US specifically and the West as a whole has lost its edge, that is due to its miscalculations on political Islam and China respectively. Added to that are problems emanating from economic, social, demographic and political trends that have been long in the making. Social trends have also been driving greater nationalism and insularity in the West. Immigration, when combined with policies promoting income disparity, has fuelled an anti-globalization narrative. As cultural nationalism spiked, the West also turned on itself: the UK on Europe and the US on its alliance commitments.

Where Europe is concerned, there has anyway been a sustained global retrenchment following the Eurozone crisis. In large measure, Europe withdrew politically from Asia, defining its interests primarily in economic terms. But the pace of change in the last decade has been so sharp that it soon found itself on the defensive even on its home turf. The comfort that the Atlantic alliance long provided has also now come into question. So, we have a picture of some turmoil and disarray. Gaps between the US and Europe are apparent on many issues even as Europe itself stands divided after years of promoting internal unity. Indeed, matters have reached a state where one could well ask whether the idea of a cohesive Western world is tenable any more. The glue which bound this framework together was the US. As that country now turns increasingly inwards, this is threatening to come unstuck. What we may therefore be seeing is an emerging multipolarity within the West. When such a West engages India, or the other way around, it is going to be different from the days when its solidarity was stronger.

India may be a rising power but it clearly still has a great distance to go. There are, however, lessons from contemporary history that it can take into account. The fact is that the most impressive growth stories of the last 150 years have all been with the participation of the West. This was true of Japan in the nineteenth century and after 1950, of South Korea in the 1960s, of the ASEAN in the 1970s and of China in the 1980s and thereafter. Even the Soviet Union had Germany as a critical partner in the 1920s to industrialize rapidly. In China's case, it reaped a double benefit from a double risk – going first with the USSR in the 1950s and then switching to the West in the 1980s. It goes without saying that the West would have its own agenda in doing so. But for its partners, the challenge is to utilize that option and handle its consequences.

What India stands to gain is fairly obvious. A stronger partnership with the West will lead to considerable political benefits and economic gains, though both would have to be balanced by Indian equities in competing constituencies. Looking just beyond the horizon, there are also immense opportunities to be exploited in terms of technology applications and human resources optimization. Globalization may currently be under some stress due to some distortions, but it will manifest itself in a revised form. While it can be asserted with some confidence that a combination of economics, technology and demographics will draw India and the West closer, the real difference would be made by politics and values. For it to succeed in good measure, India and the West must fit into each other's scheme of the world. Envisaging India's growth as a strategic development in the larger Western interest is a starting point. Such thinking has become more accepted in the US and Japan; it still has to develop more in Europe.

From an economic perspective, it would also be in the Western interest that India emerge more rapidly as a source of greater global demand and supply, thereby reducing excessive dependence on any single geography. This is going to be particularly important as we move to greater technology reliance. Given that resource and cost optimization will remain guiding principles of business, the salience of India's human resources to the global economy will only grow with time. Its market economy and responsible governance makes it a safe partner when it comes to contract designing and manufacturing.

For the West, there are also larger principles to prove in ensuring India's success. It will affirm that democratic politics and high growth economics are not mutually exclusive. India's multi-faith society is also an enormous contribution to global stability. In fact, that is what acts as a firewall preventing the spread of fundamentalism and radicalism from India's West to its East. But it also has its activist aspects that would be of growing value to a Western world. In areas like maritime security in the Indian Ocean or building connectivity in Asia, its contribution can make a difference. A willingness to shoulder greater HADR responsibility is already visible in the last few years. Its participation strengthens export control regimes dealing with sensitive technologies. And its presence not only adds to the credibility of various global initiatives and negotiations but often, as in the case of Paris on climate change, helps to find an outcome. For a Western system that must reinvent itself to stay strong, it is a good option to partner.

For all this to work, a number of important relationships need to come together in a self-supporting manner. These include India's ties with the US, the UK, Europe and Japan. When it comes to the US, it is noteworthy that India has solidified ties continuously with successive administrations in the recent past. The way forward has been to find a commonality that resonates: with Clinton, it was pluralism and business; with Bush, it was democracy and global strategy; and with Obama, climate change and radicalization. Following Trump's election, it is bilateralism, trade and security convergences. It is to India's advantage that an American President is less a prisoner of those regimes and orthodoxies that have long blocked progress with a newer partner. In the Trump vision of the world, allies have disappointed America and competitors have cheated it. India is fortunate in being neither.

The Indo-American relationship is obviously at the heart of the overall approach to the West. In its early stages, the British had a disproportionate role in crafting the larger policy. As a result, a lot of the post-Partition considerations have been carried over into foreign policy positions. Over time, however, American interests acquired a more autonomous basis that coincided with the overlaps created by India's own growing equities to the East. Even today, the differential between the convergences East and West of India are visible. How much they would diminish will reflect the larger Western closeness to India.

As the Goldilocks period with the US came to an end, efforts to expand ties yielded results. The breadth of contacts and the ease of conversations now would not have been imaginable a decade and half ago. The strength of the relationship can veritably be measured in G2G, B2B, P2P or even T2T (technology to technology) terms. A country that did not buy any military equipment for four decades operates multiple platforms now. Societal contact has been especially strong, underpinned by the large presence of Indian students. Public sentiment in both nations is very positive and the Indian diaspora has become an extraordinary bridge that has impacted the US Congress in particular.

While this relationship has undoubtedly been the transformational story of our generation, it is not without its challenges. This is inbuilt into the nature of international relations, some from diverging geopolitical perspectives and others from domestic compulsions. Currently, frictions on trade and concerns on mobility require the greatest attention. But beyond that, there is a larger issue of continuously tending to the relationship. India has to maintain a narrative in the US of its value, whether it is in terms of geopolitics, shared challenges, market attractions, technology strengths or burden-sharing. And it must be customized for the President of the day. Given the discontinuity in American policy, it is also important that their engagement continuously factors in the updated priorities and the issues that emerge from them.

The world is indeed very different, but its fundamentals have not been completely overturned. It is certainly true that Asia has risen impressively, and that the West has yielded space economically and politically. But to discount the West – Europe, leave alone the US – would be serious folly. And to suggest that growing Asian GDPs would translate themselves quickly into strategic influence is delusional. Such economic determinism may be an effective motivational exercise, but cannot serve as a basis for policymaking. The fact is that right now, the major markets are still in the West, as in fact is the capital needed for growth. More importantly, the West continues be the main source of technology and innovation, even if its leads are eroding. Global institutions are anchored in its mores as standards are largely set there. The global commons are largely regulated by the West and its invisible influence is perhaps even more potent than its visible form.

Declarations of its impending demise, therefore, are premature, to say the least. The military balance brings out this reality even more sharply. Defence budgets of the world are heavily dominated by Western expenditure, even if one excludes the US. And consider the wars fought in the last twenty-five years: Yugoslavia, Afghanistan, Iraq, Libya and Syria. Whatever their causes or results, all of them have seen a Western will to use force, great improvements in technology and its application, and a pronounced ability to apply political pressure. The US and Europe still remain the leading suppliers of military and dual-use technologies. Large parts of the world have a Western presence and they are often early responders when their interests are involved. And not coincidentally, they are the principal intermediaries in any regional negotiation.

When making a case for understanding with the West, there are understandably arguments of caution in India that reflect our difficult history. More recent developments like Iraq in 2003 and Afghanistan after 1979 are also factors, as indeed are memories of Western actions in our immediate neighbourhood. But as India rises in a more structurally loose world, this is increasingly a legacy issue. Concerns emanate from an era when India was weaker and the gap with the West much greater. Other nations were the poles of the world order and our task was to manage them with the least damage. What may have held true in the 1950s, when India chose to be non-aligned, is perhaps less so today. Maintaining that the risks have not changed since then is to dismiss the considerable achievements that India has to its record since the 1990s. It is also to underplay India's visibly improved standing in the world.

In the past, we drew a line when it came to make or break issues like the CTBT or TRIPS. Today, India has both the ability to work confidently with the West when required and differ with it when its interests so demand. Afghanistan, Iran, Russia, climate change, connectivity or terrorism are some relevant examples. Nor did India hesitate to chart its own course when occasion arose in regions like Africa. In its own neighbourhood, there has not only been a willingness to take positions, but also some ability to influence the international community by doing so. This may make it uncomfortably independent at times, but still a partner that has growing value in a more multiaxial world.

While Indians look at the future with confidence, they should not forget that the journey ahead has obstacles of history to surmount. Although it made very substantial contributions in the First and Second World Wars, India was not on the high table in 1945 and continues to pay the price of being absent. Underlining its sacrifices in these wars and subsequent peacekeeping operations is part of the endeavour to make its claims more forcefully. For all the talk of a more contemporary world order, it is evident that the entrenched powers will not readily give up their privileges, even if that means a more dysfunctional international system. Practices and regimes that derive from 1945 impinge on India negatively, whether it is the Nuclear Non-Proliferation Treaty or, till recently, representation in the International Court of Justice. Questioning the 1945 order is important but a task to be handled with considerable delicacy. It should be done with a forward-looking perspective that would appeal to the decolonized world, rather than be seen as a backward step that reverses historical outcomes. As India goes up in the international order, it will advance its own narratives, and, on occasion, question Western ones.

The fact that India is a working democracy established under the most challenging conditions should hold some clues to its nature. Whether this pluralism emanates from more recent political experiences or is an inherent cultural attribute is irrelevant. There is a sufficiently long record to suggest an ingrained respect for rules and norms. Certainly, this is the self-image, which itself is a powerful motivation. Through its actions and messaging, India has patiently created the narrative of a responsible democratic power. Few would contest that this is anything but a net asset to a world uncertain of its future directions. But there is also the fact that the evolution of the

Indian polity has brought out its societal characteristics more sharply than before. As it begins to define itself more clearly, there would be an inevitable period of argumentation and adjustment. Debates generated by the political developments of the last year indicate that this process won't be easy. At the end of the day, it will all be about rebalancing, as that is what nationalism in global affairs is hastening.

At the core of a contemporary compact with the West is the need for an appreciation of the changes in our country. This will require an acceptance that an elite created in a Western mould has now outlived its relevance. Looking beyond orthodoxies is more widely accepted now and the Munich Security Conference 2020 tellingly focused on 'Westlessness'. For its part, India must make the most of this concern while developing a nuanced understanding of the Western world. It is now values and strategy that could bring India and the West together, rather than habits and culture. How effectively that would happen will be one of the factors shaping the global landscape.

6

The Nimzo-Indian Defence

Managing China's Rise

———

'The wise win before the fight, while the ignorant fight to win'

— ZHUGE LIANG

The ability of India and China to work together could determine the Asian century. Equally, their difficulties in doing so may well undermine it. Given this combination of promise and challenges, their ties are without doubt one of the most consequential relationships of our times. The rest of the world may appreciate the remarkable rise of China; but India lives with it up close as an immediate neighbour. China has long been a big factor in its strategic calculations, more so today than ever before. These are two civilizational polities whose near-parallel journey to become modern states has not been without frictions. Getting China right is critical to India's prospects. And that is precisely why the debate on the relationship must go beyond traditional assumptions and set arguments.

History and geography make India-China relations grapple with multiple sets of realities: those of the distant past and the nearer one, of modern history and contemporary politics, of their twin but differential rise, and of the emerging future. In aggregate, they shape a complex matrix in which the world is developing a growing interest. The balance between the many faces of the relationship will determine its overall character.

The first reality pertains to centuries of tradition of strong intellectual, religious and commercial contacts. This was the era of the real Silk Road, one that was inter-penetrative, pluralistic and mutually enriching. It covered diverse routes that connected the heartland of the two civilizations and its driving force was a powerful combination of ideas and trade. For much of this period, Buddhism was the vehicle which carried numerous passengers to the benefit of all the stops on the routes. Kuche and Khotan in today's Xinjiang were the hubs of a flow from India that reached the very centre of China then. Rulers of these kingdoms along the road had Sanskrit names that testified to their connection with India. By the third century, there were even a large number of Indian families settled in Dunhuang and an equally impressive presence of monasteries en route. Kashmir was initially the focal point for shared knowledge and later paved the way for the great university of Nalanda. While this was the main artery between India and China, it was not the only one. The valleys of Brahmaputra, Chindwin and Irrawaddy were an eastern connect and the chronicles of the explorer Zhang Qian testify to a Southern Silk Road that led from Sichuan from India. There was also a sea route, first through Tonkin and then to Canton, that connected directly from peninsular India. The presence of Indian temples as far east as the Fujian coast opposite Taiwan underlines how pervasive our contacts were with China.

This deep cultural association is reflected vividly in key cultural sites of China such as the Dunhuang Caves or the White Horse Temple in Luoyang. The tradition of contacts naturally had human expressions – from those like the monks Kasyapamatanga and Dharmaraksha who brought scriptures to Luoyang, to Kumarajiva who introduced many Buddhist texts into Chinese, and Dammo/Bodhidharma who is associated with the Shaolin tradition. That the two most famous Chinese travellers through history – Fa Xian and Xuan Zang – both came to India speaks of its salient place in ancient China. The trade of that period has been the subject of extensive research and it could comfort some that it had a different balancing problem. It is said that by the sixth century, Indian music was supposedly so popular that an imperial edict sought briefly to ban it. To those who argue that there is a long tradition of productive contacts and beneficial coexistence, the record certainly backs it up. But how the cultures may have influenced each other historically has receded completely from the popular narrative.

On the Indian side, neither public sentiment about China nor awareness of these links was particularly strong. And the advocates of bonding were, in any case, rare voices. Part of that may be due to an oral tradition that kept little record of interface with others. It could equally be a reflection of a more self-centred society for whom those who left were inconsequential, and those who came but marginal. This Indian attitude towards China stands in contrast to much of the world and one not easy for the Chinese to comprehend. Today, with the popularity of Indian films or the promotion of tourism, there is the possibility of drawing on this phase of ties.

The near past initially held out some hope, expressed by the great scholar P.C. Bagchi,* that the experiences of the Second World War would bring together the two peoples who had almost forgotten their common past. Interestingly, the Chinese elite after 1949 was quite conversant with this history with India. It was telling that Chairman Mao himself reminded the Indian Ambassador in 1950 of a popular saying that Chinese who do good in this lifetime would get reincarnated in India in the next. The concept of Western Heavens, the land of Lord Buddha's birth, ran deep in Chinese society, as did the fame of the *Journey to the West* on Xuan Zang's travels. At the same time, a narrative had also developed that India's social system was inherently

---

* P.C. Bagchi, *India and China: A Thousand Years of Cultural Relations* (New Delhi: Munshiram Manoharlal, 2008).

flawed and lacking in societal cohesion. Nationalist sentiment in China saw India as compromising with Western liberalism, oblivious to its own emulation of competing ideologies.

Yet, anti-colonial feelings did lead to strong and persistent advocacy of Indian independence by China's leadership of that period. It went to the extent of vitiating their relationship with the British, especially with Winston Churchill. The role played by India as a rear base during the Second World War and the supply lifeline over the Himalayas enhanced this sense of affinity. Although this aspect receded in its prominence after 1949, new variants of the fraternity of the oppressed carried it forward. The saga of Dr Kotnis, an Indian leftist who died leading a medical mission during the Second World War, gained currency in both societies. Even the visit of India's national poet, Rabindranath Tagore, acquired positive political symbolism because of his opposition to Japanese militarism. Contemporary records may actually indicate a more mixed reception, but then history has usually been embellished by politics.

The afterglow of independence that created the basis for a Third World and lit up the Bandung Conference was the zenith of this phase. This narrative maintained its legs for a whole decade because it was politically advantageous for both nations to project a brotherhood. Its message of anti-imperialism fitted in with the Afro-Asian solidarity that the 1955 conference promoted to strengthen their standing with regard to the West. So too did a bilateral discourse that encouraged Indians to see Maoist China in more liberal terms than reality warranted. A sense of being on the same side of history contributed to working closely in international forums and of India standing up for China against the West. Its persistent advocacy of PRC representation at the UN was noteworthy, ironical given China's subsequent lack of reciprocal support for India's permanent membership of the Security Council. India was of use to China on both the Korean and Vietnam wars and the warning to the Americans of China preparing to enter the Korean War was conveyed through the Indian Ambassador in Beijing. Indian positions in global negotiations, such as on the Japanese Peace Treaty, brought out its calculations in respect of China.

The 1950s were certainly a period of camaraderie between the two nations and pictures of their leaders together convey that strongly. It was, of course, a relationship that served China, the more diplomatically isolated of the two countries then, much better. On the whole, despite the growing border differences, India was a real believer in this phase of ties. Underneath, however, there were latent tensions that were building as their transition to nation states advanced. These were to eventually feature prominently in a Sino-Soviet polemic that motivated the Chinese leadership in a way that only Communists can comprehend. The phase ended as all these issues came to a head simultaneously.

While there may be a positive recollection that still serves political convenience, it does not erase the beliefs of this period that have struck roots. Chinese nationalism had already generated a comparative history that attributed weaknesses to Indian society. To that was added now the view of democracy as apparently lacking in discipline and fortitude. These caricatures were hardly the basis for an easy equilibrium as the two societies embarked on their individual journeys of development. However, the second set of realities is valuable because they can be evoked whenever there is a mutual desire to find common ground. In fact, the coming together at the BRICS or the Shanghai Cooperation Organization is very reminiscent of this period. For all their issues with each other, India or China have at the back of their mind a feeling that they are also contesting an established Western order. They can conveniently pull out this positive view of their history whenever it suits them.

If there is indeed a history that still counts, it is the modern one. And that, truth be told, is not an easy inheritance. This third set of realities encompasses the difficult aspects of the ties, as the first flush of engagement gave way to hard security and competitive politics. It was inevitable that once they emerged as independent states establishing their borders, India and China would have to come to terms with each other. Even otherwise, it would have been a challenge to arrive at a compromise. But as this problem got entangled with China's management of Tibet, its polemics with the Soviet Union, and disputes within, events took an altogether different turn.

The issue, at the end of the day, was neither of better border claims nor of historical evidence. Nor indeed are individual incidents, however serious, the cause of the conflict. It was the politics of the period – within China, between China and India, and between China and the USSR, quite apart from the Chinese evaluation of Nehru – that precipitated a confrontation. Nehru himself realized part of that when he candidly confessed that the issue with China was not so much about territory as about domination. What he perhaps underestimated was the intensity of responses from a polity more given to use of force. Or a 'facts on the ground' approach that an argumentative society found truly difficult to comprehend.

The judgements of the period leading to the border conflict are an industry by themselves. But aspects that need closer scrutiny include whether forcing an earlier boundary negotiation in 1950 would have been beneficial to India. Or indeed, if the 1954 agreement on Tibet was a triumph of hope over calculation.

On both sides, decisions made six decades ago still have repercussions today.

From the Indian viewpoint, political and military events of that era contributed to a larger mistrust of China. That still colours public perceptions heavily and this legacy only gets oxygen from newer controversies. As the power differential increased in the last two decades, these attitudes returned to haunt the relationship. The Chinese perhaps don't realize how lasting the impact of the 1962 conflict has been on Indian public opinion. Indian minds do not have the same ability to move on that the Chinese have shown in respect of their own conflicts with Russia or Vietnam. The loser in the 1962 conflict was not just India but the relationship itself. As every new border face-off revives these memories, what should have receded from public focus actually remains ensconced there.

Some of the difficulties in the modern relationship also emanate from China's handling of Tibet and its reading of India's reaction. Evidence, even in the public domain, supports the assertion that the situation developed in a manner that was not foreseen by either nation. There is no doubt that the ensuing concern contributed thereafter to the hardening of positions on the border issue. Since then, the protagonists have seen an endurance that they may not have expected of the other.

The complicating impact of domestic politics on the relationship was obviously not restricted to the Chinese side. In India too, diplomatic options became increasingly constricted as public and political passions rose higher. Today's generation would be surprised at the extent to which they constrained decision-making in the run-up to the conflict. A look back at the 1960 visit of Premier Zhou Enlai is particularly instructive.

The other big issue that shapes the narrative of this period is China's relationship with Pakistan. The origins of this friendship are worth revisiting, because an understanding of the past provides insights to its future. An authoritative account* of these ties asks why a relationship that otherwise lacks a bond of cultural affinity or common values – normally the basis for alliances – has outlasted the test of time and global changes. Its answer is worth reflecting on. China obviously is essential for Pakistan to address a power imbalance in relation to India, especially after Western powers showed declining enthusiasm for that goal. And Pakistan, in turn, is useful for China as it transitions from being a regional power to a global one. It not only helps keep India within the South Asia box but also provides a pathway to the Islamic world. As time passed, new reasons kept emerging that gave these ties further contemporary relevance. Shared interests in the Afghan theatre was one and maritime ambitions another.

If India did not see this coming when it first did, it could only be in allowing the first principles of balance of power to be clouded by nobler goals of a better world. It is worth recalling that these ties warmed up even as the 1962 border conflict with India loomed. Once they did, it took full advantage of the contiguity that India's incomplete actions in Jammu and Kashmir allowed. To appreciate the rapidity of its development, it should be noted that as late as 1959, when India had its first major clash with China, President Ayub Khan was also talking of repelling Chinese territorial incursions. Yet by early 1962, the two nations were discussing their de facto meeting point and Pakistan actually transferred Indian territory to China in 1963. At that time, it was a gold card member of two Western alliances – SEATO and CENTO. It also hosted an American base in Peshawar and was deeply involved in Western intelligence operations. This alliance became in due course a story of high stakes and daring

---

* Andrew Small, *The China-Pakistan Axis: Asia's New Geopolitics* (London: Hurst, 2015).

policy options. But the shift in 1963 has fundamentally shaped Chinese thinking since then. Cooperation intensified and even gave Pakistan some misplaced hopes of Chinese support during the 1965 and 1971 conflicts with India.

The contemporary phase of their ties saw many of these very issues evolve further. There has been a longstanding debate in India on how it is perceived by China. Pakistan provides an answer to that calculation. But this concern was dampened at the end of the 1980s, when India and China were focusing on repairing the breaches of the past. It had taken fourteen years after the 1962 war for ambassadorial relations to be restored in 1976. Now it took twelve more for a Prime Minister of India, Rajiv Gandhi, to travel to China in 1988. The focus was on normalizing ties and stabilizing the border, objectives largely achieved over the next decade. The peace and tranquillity agreements signed in 1993 and 1996 represented the logical follow-through of these goals.

For both nations, the events leading up to 1988 were a long-awaited correction. India had improved its ties with the US through the 1980s and was concerned at the adverse fallout of the Soviet invasion of Afghanistan. The revival of Pakistan's alliance with the US was deeply detrimental to its interests. Though closely involved in the Afghan jihad, China was noting as it unfolded a weakening USSR with an amenable leadership. Improved bilateral ties were in the interest of both India and China at this juncture, as neither saw the other as a dominant concern. Economically, the two societies were broadly on par, though China had some inherent strengths that were still to kick in. Politically, of course, China had a clear edge, partly because of the 1962 outcome, but also as its alliance with the West was now really paying off. Still, it was a meeting of considerable promise for a frozen and troubled relationship. Subsequent events were to reveal that it was also one of significant misreading by India.

The events of the early 1960s had brought out the geopolitical nature of the relationship that was accentuated by ideological differences. China has already displayed stark realpolitik in its handling of India by swiftly reaching out to Pakistan. In the quarter century thereafter, Indo-Soviet relations had developed, as indeed had Sino-Pakistan ties and Sino-US collaboration. At first glance, a balance appeared to have been reached by the mid-1970s that now allowed forward movement between India and China. But rather than allow a natural equilibrium to set in, China made a policy move that was no ordinary one. What it did has been rightly described as the 'ultimate gift' one nation can give to another in modern times.

The assistance to make nuclear weapons had been extended till then only by the US to the UK, the USSR to China (before ending it half-way), and France to Israel. This short list highlights how rarely this option had till then been exercised in international relations, obviously for good reasons. The logic of the Chinese move now was in consonance with the 1963 objective – to keep Pakistan hyphenated to India. But the act carries such a premium that it answers the query of how much India really counts in Chinese calculations.

Its impact on policy and public attitudes in India were to be profound. Significantly, Sino-Pakistani nuclear collaboration starts around the time India and China revived ambassadorial-level ties between them. This compulsion by the more powerful partner to assuage the concerns of the weaker one has remained a persistent strain in Chinese thinking about Pakistan. As this tie-up assumed serious proportions, China's nuclear technology was transferred to that country even as Sino-Indian boundary negotiations picked up. The pattern continued, and the Rajiv Gandhi visit was followed by the transfer of missiles. There were even rumours of a nuclear test conducted for Pakistan by China on its soil. The story carries on and the entry of North Korea as a third party only added to its complex texture.

This set of legacy issues is a cross that Sino-Indian relations carry to this day. They not only shaped the past but remain factors that affect the present and the future. Being in denial of their implications serves little purpose. Those committed to taking forward ties must accept these realities and work through them in the interest of a larger goal. It is only by confronting a difficult history honestly that it can be really set to rest.

While the maintenance of peace and tranquillity after a conflict is no mean achievement, the boundary question acquired greater prominence as ties improved. Understandably, it was seen as key to a full normalization of ties and a step that would strengthen both parties with regard to the world. However, the two sides could not grasp the opportunities that came their way. Foreign Minister Atal Bihari Vajpayee made an earnest effort in 1979 that ended up undermined by the Chinese attack on Vietnam. Thereafter, interest was reaffirmed by Deng Xiaoping himself on multiple occasions, but never realized concretely. However, with China's modernization gathering pace and with India sliding into domestic troubles, that country made a policy change of some consequence. In characterizing the eastern sector as the main area of dispute, China went back on the positions taken by Zhou Enlai before the 1962 conflict and by Deng Xiaoping after it. Its implications for the boundary negotiations were long-lasting. Even though the political parameters and the guiding principles for a boundary settlement were eventually worked out in 2005, this changed focus created a new conundrum.

With the end of the Cold War, the overall political atmosphere changed for the better, despite the boundary dispute and the nuclear collaboration with Pakistan. Moves towards normalization gathered further pace, notwithstanding India's 1998 decision to finally go nuclear. By 2003, the establishment of the Special Representatives mechanism showed a genuine desire for a breakthrough on the border dispute. It also saw some progress on the boundary negotiations and considerable optimism on trade. China was designated as a strategic partner and there was serious thinking about a free trade agreement. Climate change and the Doha Round of trade negotiations provided the basis to make common cause in the global arena. The BRICS process, starting in 2006, affirmed a sense of non-Western bonding and briefly, Indian diplomacy seemed to be making the best of all worlds.

There were, however, signs even during this period of the influence of larger events. In 1998, the US and China came together to oppose India's nuclear tests vehemently. But it did not proceed further as adept Indian diplomacy cut its own deal with the US. However, what it did during Clinton's second term was to encourage a Chinese interest in forging a G-2 like arrangement, especially in respect to South Asia. This approach was to return under Obama, not coincidentally with the same set of American officials. Ironically, China in the 1960s used to complain about this very kind of big power condominium.

The Chinese interest in South Asia, as a whole, also expanded during this period, as did its ties with Myanmar. Anti-piracy patrols after 2008 gave it a good reason to start operating in the Indian Ocean. The establishment of ports in Pakistan and Sri Lanka had their own resonance. All the while, its higher economic growth widened the power differential with a neighbour whose commitment to reform was more half-hearted.

The year 2009 is the turning point in China's current rise. The combination of a global financial crisis, a change in the US Administration, and the consequences of the Iraq war now no longer made it necessary to hide its light. To the extent it did till 2012, this was the caution of old habits and experiences. Coming in to Beijing at that very time as Ambassador, I had a ringside view of the vigorous expression of this newfound confidence. It was visible in policy, articulation and political choreography. All nations were impacted, however differently. The ASEAN witnessed moves on the South China Sea and an accompanying change in attitude to regional structures. With Japan, there was a greater focus on its territorial dispute. The US too was tested on a range of security and economic issues. The equation with Russia shifted in China's favour and the Eurozone crisis gave an easy entry into a difficult market. With India, this period saw both bilateral challenges despite multilateral cooperation. Stapled visas and border intrusions dominated news, even as the two continued to make common cause in many global councils. With the 18th Party Congress, India's ties, like that of the rest of the world, entered a new era.

When relations were normalized by Prime Minister Indira Gandhi in 1976, the ties naturally had little economic content. Even when Rajiv Gandhi visited China a decade later, its economic content was minuscule. China's own energies were directed largely at the developed economies from whom it imported capital and technology, obtaining increasing market access in return. But as China's economy grew and India's opened up, opportunities for trade began to be more aggressively exploited. Trade figures tell their own story, growing fifty-fold in two decades. Clearly, China's entry into WTO made a big difference, as indeed did the expanding demands of India's growth. The intensely competitive nature of the Indian market that puts such a premium on price points saw a natural value in imports from China. This applied in the case of infrastructure building, especially in power generation and telecommunications, where it was also supported by attractive financing.

The Indian system did not develop the requisite standards and regulations that should normally accompany the opening of an economy. It allowed Chinese goods in to the extent of hollowing out many sectors of its own industry. Unfortunately, at the other end, there was not even a semblance of reciprocity, even in sectors like pharmaceuticals and IT services where India has a global reputation. As a result, China's exports to India are more than four times what it imports from it.

The initial advocacy in India of more trade with China has now given way to strong resentment at its one-sidedness. It is no longer confined to policy circles but shapes the perception of industry and the public. This issue has also had a vitiating impact on larger discussions. It is, therefore, a challenge that cannot wait, either in itself or for its greater significance. There seem no ready answers, but this does not justify the unhappy status quo. The twin compulsions in India of externalizing and digitizing are likely to give these issues a much sharper edge in times to come.

The prospect of a deeper economic collaboration between India and China is a complicated one. On the one hand, two of the largest economies of the world could do more business with each other, especially taking into account supply chains. On the other, this is difficult to insulate from their basic socio-economic make-up. It is not that competitive sources cannot be used to expand trade or build infrastructure and other capacities. After all, China did that itself with Japan and the West. But the Indian controls are less effective and such cheap imports in fact undercut the growth of its domestic capacities. Nor has India shown the skills of China in absorbing technologies and creating its own. This will therefore remain a vexing issue for foreseeable future. Like the rest of the world, India too is finding it difficult to come to terms with a state capitalist model that has no precedent.

Since 1963, China has refined its approach towards the Indian Subcontinent. As its economic might and political influence grew, so did its presence in India's neighbours, with all its attendant implications. For a nation that is so sensitive to developments in its own periphery, there has been little interest in addressing the natural concern of others in a similar situation. The relationship with Pakistan, in particular, has taken a quantum leap with the unfolding of the so-called China Pakistan Economic Corridor (CPEC). That this so-called corridor openly violates Indian sovereignty makes it even more unacceptable. While Sino-Pakistan collaboration is itself not recent, that cannot be said for the defence of Pakistan's more egregious actions. Blocking the sanctioning of self-confessed terrorists is taking place in isolation from the rest of the international community. It is a message that has naturally resonated negatively in India. At some stage, there could be a realization that this association with the worst face of Pakistan has its reputational costs. Until then, it will probably continue to cast its shadow.

The impact of a more powerful China will naturally be felt most on its immediate neighbourhood. In many cases, that also happens to be the periphery of India. The equilibrium between India and China is not going to be arrived at only bilaterally. It would also be shaped in different ways across a larger landscape. For India, this means stepping up its game in areas like connectivity and development projects. It has powerful cards in the form of geography, culture and societal contacts. How well it uses them all will be a real test of its strategy.

Any response obviously has to be predicated on the realization that greater ambitions and capabilities usually create a different behavioural pattern. Therefore, India too needs to think out of the box and find more creative methods of protecting its equities. If there is now an Indian willingness to break new ground, much of that derives from this perception. Interestingly, India's sense of independence is susceptible to exploitation in this regard. Words of caution that selectively draw on history can strike a chord with constituencies that are insecure. It is, therefore, essential that India has a clear-eyed view of its own interests and fashions its choices accordingly. In fact, the contemporary politics of China provides more than its fair share of lessons. At various times, it has concluded understandings with different powers to advance its rise. But emulating that is not easy for a polity like India that is characterized by greater consistency and caution. The issue, however, could end up as one less of principles than of practice.

Even in 1971, when India moved closer to the USSR, it did so in response to a new geopolitical development – the Sino-US rapprochement. By concluding the Indo-Soviet Treaty, it actually safeguarded its freedom of action rather than compromise it. Today, there is a new geopolitical challenge – the emergence of multipolarity. It surely does not call for a response as drastic as 1971, but definitely encourages a widening of India's options and understandings. The objective is to create a better balance and working closely with converging interests. As China itself has demonstrated, working with others is an integral element of an upward trajectory. Only those who lack self-confidence will doubt the wisdom of doing so. It is important that India not be either persuaded nor pressurized to restrict its options.

A rising China seeks to shape Asia, perhaps even the world, to its architectural vision. Many of its key plans are unilateral enterprises. The Belt and Road Initiative (BRI) appears to serve its national objectives and conscious collaboration is naturally for those who envisage convergence with those goals. The issue is not about connectivity in itself; there is an obvious paucity of that in a continent distorted by colonial history. India has supported a range of initiatives within the country, in its South Asian and maritime periphery, to South-East Asia and to West Asia and beyond. But these are all consultative endeavours based on broadly accepted commercial principles and goals. India is comfortable with the connectivity contributions of the Asian Infrastructure Investment Bank and the BRICS New Development Bank. China has a key role in both institutions.

A concern arises when there is a departure from norms and transparency, that too to serve a limited agenda. In May 2017, India took the lead in the global debate on connectivity. It stated publicly that connectivity initiatives must be based on universally recognized international norms, good governance, rule of law, openness, transparency and equality. They must also follow principles of financial responsibility to avoid projects that would create unsustainable debt burdens for communities. They should uphold balanced ecological and environmental protection and preservation standards, transparent assessment of project cost and transfer skills and technology to help the running and maintenance of assets created by local communities. Not least, India emphasized that connectivity projects must be pursued in a manner that respects sovereignty and territorial integrity. Clearly, concerns about the so-called China-Pakistan Economic Corridor and experiences in its periphery shaped India's position. Since then, the global conversation on connectivity has expanded, much of it in line with India's thinking.

It is actually the final set of realities between India and China that are going to be critical: when China is really becoming global and India, at the same time, is moving towards a bigger role in world affairs. Reconciling their aspirations and interests will require maturity of leadership in both nations, as well as the systemic skills of diplomacy. The established set of historical issues, especially border differences, will probably continue to influence the nature of the ties. Their impact on public perception of China is only growing with the passage of time. But new variables could also enter the calculation, some more benign, others less so. A lot will depend on how consciously and effectively both countries steer the relationship into more positive domains. Those who have a better visualization of what is at stake will obviously support such endeavours.

Getting used to each other's larger footprint will not be easy for either nation. Just as China seeks to raise its profile in South Asia, India too will gradually do so in South-East Asia and East Asia. The maritime domain, by its nature, will be particularly given to such activities. India is used to thinking of China only to the North; its presence in the South will mean something else. But this is also an arena where India holds some geographical, historical and cultural advantages.

As they both rise, albeit at a differential rate and from an uneven start, much would depend on perceptions of each other's attitudes. What it could boil down to is an overall sense of whether each is sufficiently accommodative of the other's rise. From India's perspective, how open China will be to its permanent membership of the UN Security Council will be one factor. The opportunity for text-based negotiations could provide an answer. Membership of the Nuclear Suppliers Group is another indicator, as it reflects both India's arrival as a technology player and puts behind an obsolete framework. There would be many more occasions as new regimes, mechanisms and situations emerge.

When they look beyond just national interest, the two countries are indeed convergent in their effort to create a more balanced world. Be it in ensuring a strong and stable Russia, an Africa with more choices, or in preventing fundamentalist inroads into their heterogeneity, their interests overlap. At international negotiations, they sometimes find themselves on the same side of the argument. In June 2017, when the leaders of the two countries met at Astana, they reached consensus that at a time of global uncertainty, India-China relations are a factor of stability and in their relationship, India and China must not allow differences to become disputes. This revealed that despite all their divergences, there is a strategic maturity at work between them. That realization led to the Wuhan and Chennai Summits of 2018 and 2019 respectively. When shorn of their optics, both occasions were exercises in pure realism. The two nations discussed their future and that of the world very much with a sense of history. So, the world should hope that this perspective will find ways of getting beyond traditional limitations.

China's powerful rise is among the multiple factors that have led to a more uncertain world. As the politics of this era evolves, neither country has an interest in allowing the other to become a card against them. Making sure of that will depend on their own policies. One concern is that unlike on the rest of world, India's rise has been partly lost on a China that has been growing five times faster. It is up to India to ensure that its enhanced standing is given due weight. What was different at Wuhan and Chennai was not just the intensity of the engagement, but its setting against the evolving global backdrop in which both have such an important role. The practice of leaders of India and China having geopolitical conversations ceased many decades ago. Its resumption could well be a sign of a different future.

As India assesses the rise of China and weighs its own achievements, it should be objective about its prospects in comparison. To begin with, whatever political rhetoric in our country suggests from time to time, there are gaps in their comprehensive national power. We have yet to build some deep capabilities, achieve human development indices or create the growth conditions that China did for the last four decades. On the contrary, we have made industrialization harder and until recently, paid inadequate attention to developing the requisite levels of capacities and skills. More relevant to global affairs,

India will not get the openness in the world economy that China enjoyed, say in 2006, when they had the same per capita income. Nor can it reach the kind of compact with global capitalism that China could in the past.

There is also a set of political factors that need to be taken into account. For most of its growth period, China faced no pressure from other powers, entrenched or rising. The Soviet challenge diluted in the 1980s and the Tiananmen concerns in the West quickly gave way to profit margins. So, politically at least, it had a good run till recently. India does not enjoy that luxury as it follows China's rise. It has the pressure of a predecessor that China did not have. And that power is a neighbour with whom there are zones of overlapping interests. Equally relevant, the world has become more careful of changing balances than in the past. India, therefore, has its task cut out for it. With less going for us, we also have a harder climb.

Given a difficult bilateral history and now a complicated global context, India's challenge is to manage a more powerful neighbour while ensuring its own rise. In doing so, there must be an understanding on our part that this search for equilibrium is an infinite process. Some issues may be amenable to an early resolution but others may not. The current situation could change and strategic calculations must not be the monopoly of China. Neither should be the willingness to take initiative. Where tested, it is essential to stand one's ground. That experience also drives home the importance of not being psychologically undermined nor allowing constituencies within to be used.

The India-China relationship will always take into account the larger context as they establish an equilibrium. World events determine not just China's overall attitude but its specific demeanour towards India. Currently, this context is dominated by global frictions and systemic differences. It is, therefore, necessary for India to continuously monitor this larger picture as it calibrates its China relationship. In setting the terms of interaction, we have also seen swings between textualism and realism, often to our detriment. Some of the historical accounts of negotiations bring out how China used inexactitude to give itself more wiggle room. At the same time, major policy changes have also been effected by simply dismissing the past. Extracting ritualistic affirmations from the other side on concerns has been one way of playing the game. India has however been more reciprocal in seeking commitments of late. Today, the bottomline for the relationship is clear: peace and tranquillity must prevail on the border if the progress made in the last three decades is not to be jeopardized. The border and the future of ties cannot be separated.

For new ground to be broken, much more is needed on the positive side of the ledger. But it is equally important to guard against unilateral actions that increase volatility. While the centrality of the border factor has been long recognized, their activities and interests in global politics will now have a greater relevance in the overall calculation. We have to distinguish here the normal interplay of nations in international politics from a more focused effort at creating an equilibrium. When the logic of power is viewed through the lens of realism, China will advance its objectives and exploit its edge. In turn, India must respond unemotionally but effectively, especially when presented with challenging situations. We have always assumed that a more substantive relationship would naturally be a more stable one. Recent trends underline that this should not be taken as a given. Instead, each should strive to occupy a greater mind space of the other.

India is not the only country focused on coming to terms with a significantly more powerful China. In fact, the entire world is doing so, each nation refashioning its terms of engagement in its own way. If there is a common approach, it is of them simultaneously strengthening capacities internally, assessing the external landscape and seeking understandings with China. In this overall exercise, India will occupy a special place by virtue of its size, location, potential, history and culture. The key to a more settled Sino-Indian relationship is a greater acceptance by both countries of multipolarity and mutuality, building on a larger foundation of global rebalancing.

In November 1950, Sardar Patel and Pandit Nehru had a famous exchange of views on how to approach China. Much has changed since, mostly to India's disadvantage. The key issues – realism versus optimism and bilateralism versus globalism – remain as relevant today as then. Striking a judicious balance is not necessarily easier with the passage of time. But the past also tells us that there is always room for strategy and vision if we are to go beyond politics and constraints. More than on any other relationship in the world today, the long view must prevail.

In chess, an 'Indian Defence' is a popular opening for those who find themselves playing black. And indeed, playing black has been the standard Indian strategic posture. As life becomes complicated, there are learnings in what Aron Nimzowitsch introduced to the game a century ago. Known as the 'Nimzo-Indian Defence', he imaginatively created latitude for the black; and therein lies a lesson.

7

A Delayed Destiny

India, Japan and the Asian Balance

———

'At the moment of victory, tighten the cords of your helmet'

— TOKUGAWA IEYASU

Asia is being shaped largely by the outlook of the US, the power of China, the weight of Russia, the collectivism of ASEAN, the volatility of the Middle East and the rise of India. If there is an underplayed element, that is in the presence of Japan. The strategic withdrawal of Japan along with the Partition of India skewed the power balance in the Asian continent. The West may be responsible for both developments, but is now recalculating in its own interest.

There are two imponderables which could create a very different scenario in Asia. One is the future posture of Japan, bringing back into the strategic calculus a major economy with enormous technological capabilities. The second is the fluidity in the Korean Peninsula, one that could overturn longstanding assumptions. Both were earlier impacted by the rising power of China. But now, they could also respond to a new American posture. For India, the first will have direct consequences, but even the second would not be irrelevant. Between them, we could well see influences from East Asia that go beyond those of China.

The issue is not just of power calculations but equally of mindsets. Neither India nor Japan had historically focused on each other when it came to addressing their respective security situations. Yet, they both think similarly on the big issues of the day, especially in the last few years. This applies to power shifts as much as power deficits. So, what strategy may not have consciously generated, the vagaries of an uncertain world may well have done. A shared interest in securing the global commons and to contributing to global goods has brought about a convergence between very different polities. This realization in two nations that they have little choice but to help shape their continent is now an impelling force of a new relationship.

In the forgotten footnotes of history are conversations between Japanese and British diplomats in 1904-05 exploring military cooperation against a Russian threat. Some British hoped that it could lead to the dispatch of Japanese troops to India. That prospect of such an army commitment in return for British naval support never materialized since Japan decisively defeated the Russians at sea in Tsushima. But what did not happen does illustrate a working principle of international relations. As two imperial powers that were proximate to the expanding Russian empire, the UK and Japan perceived a convergence of interests that lasted from the 1860s to the 1920s. This period witnessed other expressions of mutual support, including the despatch of Japanese marines to suppress an Indian mutiny in Singapore in 1915. There was even a formal Japanese military representative in India, with some of the attachés later becoming leading wartime generals. Japan was initially careful not to offend British imperial sensibilities and rejected any overtures to the contrary. It was only after this common ground eroded that it went on to become a base for Asian revolutionary activities. Remnants of this sentiment continued even after 1945, when their militaries cooperated in the attempted restoration of empires in South-East Asia. By every strategic logic, this approach should have continued. But it did not and therein lies one of the peculiarities of Asian security.

The causes for the non-strategic nature of modern India-Japan relations deserve introspection. Because, for all the ups and downs in Asia over the last seven decades, these two nations have a very limited history of policy exchanges, leave alone anything more. This distance between polities, whose natural interests should dictate otherwise, would normally be inexplicable. But we should remember that grand strategy could trump geopolitics in the era of the Cold War. Japan got drawn into the American security alliance, whereas India chose the non-alignment path. Particularly after India moved closer to the USSR, the sense of being on opposite sides of the Cold War was strong. There was, admittedly, a brief period in the late 1950s when some bonding was in evidence. But India's defeat in the 1962 border war with China diminished its standing in Japan considerably. That country was part of the Western bloc's cultivation of China after 1971 and this put India and Japan on even more divergent paths. In different ways, both harboured a fascination for China that led them to focus on that country to the exclusion of each other.

For Japan, culture was always central to the pull of China. After the war, it was also the focus of atonement for excesses. And very soon thereafter, a magnet which attracted outward-looking Japanese businesses. For India, there was the fraternity after decolonization until territorial differences made it untenable. The compulsions of a shared land border were themselves a powerful factor for intensive engagement. And in an earlier era where Western nations were busy undermining India's integrity, China was viewed more positively. That the West had also put such a premium on China inevitably influenced the thinking of both India and Japan.

China may have preoccupied India and Japan over many years in different ways. But they were even more transfixed by other immediate neighbours with whom ties were particularly difficult. One had Pakistan, the other North Korea. As a result, India and

Japan coexisted harmoniously but distantly, each in the midst of their own preoccupations. Neither saw the other as contributing to their search for solutions. Until, of course, the challenges of a volatile world created by shifting balances of power became so large that the problem itself was redefined.

When India decided to look more to the East a quarter century ago, it was the beginning of a profound correction in its foreign policy. The Western bias that was an outcome of its colonial past was strengthened by the prevailing global scenario. The two superpowers – the US and USSR – were both faces of that Western world, even if they represented competing forces. Europe also occupied a very prominent place in Indian thinking and the collective influence of the West was visible in politics, economics and security. The 1991 crisis, however, changed India's model of development and made it look more towards Asian economic growth of relatively recent origin. ASEAN served as a path of entry into this new syndrome and its institutions helped socialize India into a different world.

Since then, India's interface with South-East Asia and East Asia has grown steadily. Its economic collaborations with Japan, South Korea and China have expanded under all governments. This was also a period when Asia in general, and China in particular, was gaining greater global clout. Later, the repositioning of American power and the re-emergence of Japan were also factors to be taken into account. What started as an economic correction in India increasingly factored in these political developments and ended up more as a strategic one. Whether it is activities, transactions, challenges or attention, the centre of gravity for India has shifted much more to the East. That explains the necessity of Indo-Pacific as a working principle. India was always India, but its modern sense of being Asia has developed more strongly by looking and acting eastwards.

The phrase 'Looking East' certainly connotes a vector but has evolved into a diplomatic metaphor. Initially, it started out as an expression of India's opening out to the world after decades of relatively autarchic growth. Because our early partnerships in the 1990s were with members of the ASEAN, it then acquired a specific meaning as developing ties with them. In due course, efforts were made to establish more connectivity with that region – physical, virtual as well as its softer incarnations. Engagement with ASEAN was also reflected in India's participation in various ASEAN-centric forums. An agenda of trade, investment and economic changes thus grew steadily into something much larger. It also then went beyond ASEAN to cover Japan, the Republic of Korea and China. With the first two, India concluded free trade agreements, while with China, trade volumes expanded dramatically. In recent years, this outreach has extended to Australia and the Pacific Islands. As a result, India's foreign policy acquired a footprint and dimension that it did not have earlier. The profundity of this change is underlined by the larger mind space that the world to India's East now occupies when it comes to economics, technology, security, strategy or even culture.

While the relevance of the East to India's global positioning has been steadily increasing, it escalates sharply when there is a substantial change in the capabilities and influence of its major powers. With China, that has already happened and is beginning to be felt. With Japan, that is a prospect which is still only unfolding.

Since 1945, that country has largely tailored its security outlook to the requirements of its American alliance. That dynamic also justified Japan's assistance and investments in China, although commercial considerations and post-war obligations were also key factors. After accounting for a larger proportion of the US trade deficit than China does today, Japan stepped back in the 1980s. It consciously chose to discipline its expectations within the alliance construct. Then, having become the second biggest economy in 1987 overtaking the USSR, it yielded that place to China in 2010.

This has had both psychological and strategic implications. Neighbours are most affected by rising powers and Japan proved no exception to this rule. Its interest in ensuring continental and regional stability is today buttressed by its desire to strengthen the global commons. As it assumes greater responsibilities and builds more partnerships, it is stepping beyond its immediate past. This evolution of Japan, as it happens, has implications far beyond East Asia. It would mean the arrival of a first-class technology power among the ranks of major players.

Given its trade focus, Japan puts a premium on economic goals that far exceed what other major powers do. Since trade has been the primary driver of its rejuvenation, it understandably dominates its strategic calculations. If a country like India is looking to hedge on its security needs, Japan's similar predicament arises more in the economic domain. This is not going to be easy, particularly with pressures on global supply chains and controls on emerging technologies. Japan's challenge would be to bridge these divides to the extent possible.

Its political diplomacy runs largely parallel to these efforts, obviously giving primacy to the US as its alliance partner. To some extent, Japan's predicament is conceptually the same as that of the rest of Asia. It too is engaged in multipolar diplomacy, no longer dependent completely on others, nor oblivious to the growth around it. If there is a new Asian balance to be forged, Japan cannot be left out of that endeavour. And if ASEAN's centrality is questioned, it is difficult to stand by and just watch a grouping that Japan helped so much to create. Where connectivity is to be encouraged or maritime activity secured, these are no longer matters on which it can remain agnostic. Such situations have led Japan and India to discover each other strategically.

Even though it is coming from a very different place, India has mirror-image requirements that also compel it to look more seriously at Japan. That cooperation with Japan holds tremendous economic and even security potential has been well recognized in New Delhi. The difficulty on the economic side was to get beyond the Official Development Assistance to more substantive trade and investment. Japanese companies have long spoken of the cultural gap with India and contrasted it to the reception that they were accorded in South-East Asia and China. The pre-existence of local businesses, disciplines of a rule-based polity and sensitivity towards favouring foreign players have all been responsible for arduous progress in India. Converting a broad Japanese footprint in India into a deep one has, therefore, always been a challenge.

The two countries may have long enjoyed very cordial relations, but it also tended to be one that was low on ambition and high in rhetoric. Where politics and security are concerned, a Japan that was firmly placed in an American alliance was not easy to engage in the past. It was itself reticent and its American connection only added a further sense of distance. Both situations are today being addressed and these efforts are already bearing initial fruit. Improving ease of doing business and specially responding to the requirements of Japanese companies has also yielded encouraging results. Putting instruments in place is only the first step towards creating significant outcomes. Similarly, much closer Indian relations with the US have made it a facilitator, rather than an obstacle to India-Japan ties. In fact, the ability of India, Japan and the US to work together in a trilateral framework has been one of the novel elements of the changing Asian political landscape.

From India's viewpoint, close ties with Japan offer many benefits. To begin with, it takes India out of the South Asia box to which it has been confined since independence. It also moves it beyond South-East Asia, which is as far as the Look East policy took it. Only a partner in East Asia that encourages India to operate there and reciprocates by also maintaining a presence in the Indian Ocean makes Indo-Pacific a reality. While Japan is essential to that endeavour, others like South Korea can also have relevance. The role of the ASEAN and its individual member states as a bridge goes without saying.

Another aspect is the contemporary requirement to form loose working arrangements with convergent powers. Where Asia is concerned, this requires some countries to step forward and take on more responsibilities in areas like maritime security and connectivity building. There is, of course, the most direct benefit of the Japan relationship: its contribution to accelerate India's growth. Convincing mainstream Japan that a larger and more capable Indian economy is not just a business opportunity but also a strategic advantage is therefore essential. The challenge is for the Indian side to create conditions to ensure that this takes practical shape in the near term.

While these are all compulsions of immediate politics, it is also worthwhile to consider this relationship from the longer perspective of history. A newer generation in both countries have found a more practical logic for forging ties than the earlier lot of political romantics. The real value of Japan lies in its well-earned reputation as the great modernization leader in Eurasia. Its example and experiences have motivated other countries to follow suit and Japan itself has assisted that process. If it could really bring those energies to bear on India now, then the transformational possibilities truly expand. This has gained greater significance in recent years, because the ability of the

West to contribute to this agenda has weakened. India may not be a factor in a Japanese strategic posture, but it could well be a beneficiary. A multipolar Asia will really only come about with the participation of Japan.

In Indian politics, Japan is unique in being a relationship that has always enjoyed the distinction of support across the political spectrum. Forging ahead on this account is, therefore, likely to be the least divisive of foreign policy initiatives. Successive governments at the Centre and most state governments have shown deep interest in exploiting the Japan opening. The foundations of the current relationship were laid in 2000 by the visit to India of Prime Minister Mori. That initiative put behind it the acrimony generated by Japan's reaction to India's 1998 nuclear tests. Once the air was cleared, both sides responded steadily to the logic of cooperation. This has taken various forms in the last two decades, and includes much larger commitments of development assistance in hard and soft infrastructure. Japanese support was a crucial factor in India's recovery during the 1991 balance of payments crisis. Even recently, the impact of the currency swap agreement in 2018 underlines its indispensability as an economic partner.

While the economic content of these ties has expanded, the real change has been in the political warming up between India and Japan. Countries who saw each other some decades ago as alternative models in global affairs now found increasing common ground in changed circumstances. Bilaterally, they have initiated a range of dialogues and mechanisms that facilitate policy convergence. An ability to reach agreements in domains as sensitive as civil nuclear energy cooperation and defence equipment speaks for the growing comfort levels.

The conduct of serious military exercises annually by two nations would be no small matter in any case. Given that Japan is a partner, it is in fact exceptional progress. Far from being politically controversial, this is perceived in India as contributing to larger stability and security. The conclusion of a logistics exchange agreement, agreed to in principle in 2019, has the potential of taking cooperation to a new level. Their greater responsiveness to each other's regional concerns has been publicly expressed. Interests in non-proliferation, counterterrorism and maritime security are more visibly coordinated. The gruelling experience of seeking a revision in the composition of the UN Security Council has brought them closer. Horizons of cooperation have now expanded and even extend to third countries. Perhaps the most remarkable fact is that Japan is involved in many of the bolder diplomatic initiatives we have undertaken, including the Quad, a 2+2 foreign-defence consultation and a trilateral with Australia.

While few would have predicted that the political facet of this relationship would lead the economic one some day, it is not that the latter has really been slowing down either. Japan had traditionally made Official Development Assistance (ODA) the centrepiece of its strategy. This has been significantly expanded and, in fact, these ODA projects have been among the most successfully executed in the country in the present times. Flagship initiatives include Metro projects that have transformed urban management and the Delhi-Mumbai Industrial Corridor that can multiply industrial production. Additional freight and industrial corridors are on the drawing board and their importance to addressing India's logistical bottlenecks is significant.

On the business side, there has been a perceptible expansion in the presence of Japanese companies in India and a stronger commitment by those already there. The enabling environment for them has been significantly improved with specific initiatives to improve their living conditions and travel. More significantly, the two countries have been working on enhancing the quality of skills and training necessary for Japanese requirements. Industrial townships, training institutes, language centres and special finance facilities have been agreed upon. Their expeditious and effective implementation holds the key to scaling up of Japanese business in India. Synchronizing Foreign Direct Investment and Official Development Assistance polices could help open up more pathways that could be beneficial to both parties. A noteworthy step was the creation of an Act East Forum to promote connectivity initiatives in India's North-East region and extend that to Bangladesh and Myanmar. This reflects the maturing of economic thinking into larger strategic policy.

Japan, of course, has a longstanding presence in the Indian economy and society. But, opportunities in India that opened up a quarter century ago did not evoke the expected response due to their over-caution as much as our own uncertainties. Competing demands from other growing economies were also a factor. Nevertheless, Japan was responsible for major technological upgrades of the Indian economy. An earlier generation of Indians will recall how much the arrival of the Maruti-Suzuki cars changed not just their transport but the way of life. The next generation probably feels the same about the Delhi Metro Rail project. The real value of Japan is its ability to impact entire sectors of the economy and help create new enterprises and capabilities. Whether India will use that as effectively as China and ASEAN did remains to be seen.

The enhanced salience of Japan to the Asian calculus is significant not just in terms of added capabilities but also greater comfort. The two nations have a shared commitment to democracy, tolerance, pluralism and open society. Their common traditions also strengthen this bonding. In Japan, India sees a partner committed to a peaceful, open, equitable, stable and rule-based order in the Indo-Pacific and beyond. This combination of interests and values are the basis for a stronger convergence today. Given the range of interests that both nations have, the relationship goes beyond its bilateral facet. Their regional intersection will see cooperation as net security providers, collaborating on connectivity and harmonizing interests in third countries.

At the global level, India and Japan could collaborate on climate change, terrorism and reform of the old world order. How they factor in each other's sensitivities will say much for this transforming relationship. On its part, Japan will have to move beyond its comfort zone to come to terms with the realities of Asia. Dealing with an India is best done through bilateral diplomacy. Generating understanding of developments key to its welfare would surely come from extending support for similar Indian concerns. While partnering in an effort to reform the UN, it will also have to engage vigorously those that resist change. On India's side, expectations must be tempered by a recognition that Japan has its own compulsions and culture. While the two countries have much going for them in expanding their relationship, there is no automaticity about it. This caution is warranted because there is sometimes an assumption that Japan would see the world in terms similar to us. The fact is that we are dealing with a more deliberative society that seeks greater consensus to make decisions.

The challenges are, however, not limited to the different temperament of our societies. Expanding business is without doubt the most important goal. On the Indian side, there has to be a constant improvement of the enabling environment, a specific focus on Japanese requirements and an aggressive utilization of instruments that have been put in place. None of this is a given in a polity where the tendency has often been to benchmark itself against its own past. Indians will have to display some of the perseverance that is normally associated with Japan. On the Japanese side, there has to be more risk-taking and a stronger commitment to scale up. The longer the delay in its entry or expansion, the higher will be the cost. Rather than wait for India to produce the ideal conditions to do business, Japanese companies must take more initiative to shape it themselves. To that extent, they need to imbibe some Indian traits that would help them take the plunge.

In the political arena, India and Japan may both hedge, but not necessarily on the same issues and to the same degree. Neither has an interest in closing any option in a multipolar world, especially those in the immediate neighbourhood. How to execute that in real life without doubting each other will need attention. Even on an issue like connectivity, the compulsions of the two nations are somewhat different. A continuous dialogue is necessary, especially on issues of less convergence. As the one that is more deeply embedded in the entrenched order, Japan would also have to factor in new balances and shifts of influence. Its ability to look beyond established Western interests will be tested in such a world. The relationship will only grow if it is firmly anchored on an approach of mutual benefit.

While this is clearly a relationship where the past is not a guide for the future, there are nevertheless some lessons from near history that are worth studying. For much of their relationship, the two nations have been exceptionally generous to each other. Where India is concerned, it saw Japan's 1905 victory over Russia as the beginning of an Asian resurgence. Thereafter, its anti-colonial contribution was directly impactful on India. Even now, the Indian public associates Japan inextricably with the saga of Netaji Subhas Chandra Bose. The subsequent era only built on this legacy further. India took an independent stance with regard to the Tokyo Tribunal and Justice Radhabinod Pal is a name that still resonates in many quarters. If the waiving of reparations and Japan's entry into the Asian Games were reflective of a unique Indian approach, it was repaid in full measure by the extension of yen loans and sustained economic support from the Japanese side. This is a relationship very much based on popular goodwill and the image of Japan in India has been consistently positive, especially in bridging modernity with tradition.

As for the image of India in Japan, it had multiple facets: as a source of Buddhism, for its intellectual traditions and its rich culture. But all of this existed under a glass ceiling of low growth rates and limited socio-economic transformation. So, when the first serious test came in the form of the 1998 nuclear tests, the relationship stumbled severely. The explanation for that lies largely in the duality of a Japan reconciling its Asian character with its Western interests.

At that time, Japan not only bought the Western narrative on non-proliferation but also the hyphenation of India-Pakistan and the accompanying analysis of Jammu and Kashmir. Consequently, Japan ended up as the prime mover of measures against India, including the UN Security Council Resolution 1172. It is important to reflect on this period because there are pointers for the future direction of ties. When India and Japan have dealt directly with each other rather than through Western mediation, their instincts have been positive. Japan must surely note how pragmatic Western countries and China eventually were in the aftermath of 1998. Therefore, developing a sharper sense of geopolitics can certainly contribute to building ties with India.

India and Japan are admittedly two very different societies, each with its own distinct history, sociology and culture. In the past, their distance was accentuated by the pulls and pressures of international politics. They have no history of significant differences in the past, yet took many years to develop a substantive agenda. Their civic culture, political ethos and even hedging mentality are all very different. But shared interests, common values and global responsibility are beginning to close the previous distance. It is not just with government; even Japanese business see the value of a stronger India. Both countries are striving hard to find shared ground and have exceeded expectations in that effort. As a result, it has taken just a few years for this to be seen as the most natural strategic equation in Asia. The challenge is to make it among the more substantive ones as well. And more than that with any other major relationship, time is at a premium.

There are important lessons from Japanese history that could impinge on the future of Asia, and thus of India. From the Meiji era onwards, that country has always leveraged the international environment. It has also responded to global power equations and always found partners to improve its position. That tradition surely continues. Japan actually has an India history and its logic may unfold once global impediments are removed. The end of the Cold War and now developments in its American alliance may be relevant in that regard. After 1945, Japan did not give up on the world but chose instead to pursue influence through economic means. It did so on the basis of assumptions that may no longer be entirely valid. With a history of embracing change, it could do so again if circumstances so compel.

Japan may hold much of the potential for change, but the ASEAN remains India's gateway to the East. In fact, as it progresses in that direction, the basics of its approach must be continuously refreshed and underlined. There is a lot that India has learnt and continues to learn from that region. More than any other grouping, ASEAN has constantly adjusted to the larger global environment, even as they forged ahead with their regional integration and national progress. Through its very creation,

ASEAN had put behind it many of the post-decolonization debates of this region. It navigated the Cold War very adeptly to usher in an era of high economic growth that served as a model to others. Weathering the impact of the Asian financial crisis in 1997, it then went on to actually expand its footprint through the East Asia Summit process. All its members benefited from the more open global economic architecture and largely came through the 2008 crisis as well.

Today, however, they confront multiple stress tests and it is important that India is for them a part of the solution. The challenges they face include new power equilibriums, greater political unpredictability, issues of rules and norms, uncertain geo-economic directions, the question of internal cohesion and perhaps even of the centrality of ASEAN to Asia's future.

This is, therefore, exactly the right moment for India to expand its engagement with the group, adding dimensions like security, strengthening connectivity and doing more business. But beyond that, Indian strategic interests warrant that ASEAN's centrality is preserved, if not strengthened. All its bilateral and regional energies must be utilized to that end. Furthermore, as new concepts like Indo-Pacific gain traction, it is important that ASEAN is made to feel comfortable with them. They must be persuaded that a larger strategic domain would both conceptually and literally put them more at its centre. Similarly, mechanisms like Quad or Trilaterals should be seen visibly as supportive of ASEAN objectives. Sustained signalling to that effect is very much the need of the day.

The story of the ASEAN-India partnership started at the 1992 Singapore Summit, with India becoming a full Dialogue Partner in 1996, a Summit Partner in 2002 and a Strategic Partner in 2012. The special Commemorative Summit to mark its Silver

Jubilee brought the leaders of all ten ASEAN nations for the 2018 Republic Day celebrations in New Delhi. A message by itself, it also underlined how much this relationship had filled out during this period. Historically and culturally, the links between India and South-East Asia have been deep and profound. Expressions of shared heritage and culture are found across the region. Indeed, some of the best surviving examples of Indian civilization over the ages are there.

Even in more modern times, their destinies have been linked by global political currents that brought India back into the picture. Singapore, in fact, is a particularly telling example of how the future of contemporary India was shaped in South-East Asia during the Second World War. In the years thereafter, as they all achieved independence, ASEAN leaders cooperated and competed as they set about fashioning their national prospects. And India was a point of relative agreement compared to other powers who were more divisive.

What really changed in 1992 was that a relationship which was largely harmonious but only moderately energetic was now suddenly charged by a new economic imperative. This was, thereafter, taken forward by a series of policy initiatives, including a number of free trade agreements. Investment and trade flows between ASEAN and India have been steadily growing with Singapore as the principal hub. Businesses from this region occupy a prominent position in the Indian economy across a broad range of activities, spanning telecommunications and aviation to logistics, road building, industrial parks, and finance. On their part, Indian companies have a presence in energy, commodities, infrastructure and banking. The expansion of connectivity between India and South-East Asia is both a driver and an outcome of these collaborations. Indeed, over the last twenty-five years, the inter-penetration and travel between ASEAN and India has been so extensive that most Indians now intuitively think of this region as part of their neighbourhood.

This relationship has gone well beyond its economic and even cultural dimensions. There are thirty mechanisms between India and ASEAN, including an annual summit and seven ministerial dialogues. From the Indian perspective, ASEAN occupies a central place in the security architecture of the Asia-Pacific region. It is the considered Indian view that precisely because ASEAN represents the cultural, commercial and physical crossroads of the region, it has a unique ability to reflect and harmonize larger interests of the world beyond it. We have seen this already in the workings of the ASEAN Regional Forum (ARF), of which India became a member in 1996. There was even greater appreciation of the criticality of ASEAN to the larger continental stability when it conceptualized and implemented the East Asia Summit process. India was one of its original members and this gathering is a key event in its annual diplomatic calendar. It found considerable value in the ADMM Plus gathering of Defence Ministers as well.

The more structured processes have been buttressed by the informal and ad hoc ones as well. Among the arrangements that India works with today are the ReCAAP agreement on combating piracy in Asia and, as a funnel state, the cooperation mechanism in the Straits of Malacca and Singapore. The regional engagement is strengthened by a broad range of bilateral defence and security relationships with all members of ASEAN and, indeed, of the EAS as well. Because the ASEAN style is consensual and soft spoken, the value it brings to the table is often underestimated.

Noteworthy as this unfolding story of cooperation is, its real importance actually lies in the deeper significance that the post-1991 era has had for the reform of the Indian polity. A few years ago, there was a bumper crop of books on the 1991 economic crisis, some of them centring around Prime Minister Narasimha Rao. It was a natural occasion in India to debate the significance of those events. Tuning in from a foreign policy perspective, what came out was the critical role that ASEAN and Singapore especially played in shaping the thought processes of Indian decision makers. This was a forum for India to engage the world more expansively, test ideas, exchange views and seek feedback. Mentors of this region found a more-ready audience in a changing India. Their advice and experiences offered guidance as India moved along an uncharted path.

It was, therefore, only fitting that India acknowledged this debt through the presence of Prime Minister Modi at the funeral of Lee Kuan Yew, former Singapore Prime Minister, in 2015. Today, the changes underway in India are deeper and broader. A very determined effort is being made to expand manufacturing, transform infrastructure and enhance the quality of human resources. The formalization of the economy is also being accelerated, as indeed is the removal of impediments to its efficiency. It is highlighted by a commitment to make it easier to do business. Much of this transformation goes beyond narrow economic policies and involves social changes of differing magnitudes. Consequently, we have also seen awareness campaigns and motivational efforts to broaden public support. Some of it at least would be familiar to the ASEAN political culture.

Growing ties with ASEAN was initially described in India as our 'Look East' policy. To underline our seriousness in taking it forward, especially through physical connectivity projects, this was upgraded to 'Act East' a few years ago. This evolution also reflected its expanding security content. But whatever its name, this relationship actually reflects a profound shift in India's geopolitical outlook towards the world to its East. Contacts and cooperation with South-East Asia opened up to India the world beyond it. This was around the time when India also sought to engage Japan, South Korea and China more seriously. There is no question that ASEAN was a conduit – psychologically, politically and perhaps even physically. In the years thereafter, as we entered the East Asia Summit process, this particular direction of India's engagement strengthened even further and extends now to Australia and New Zealand as well as the Pacific Islands. Indeed, without ASEAN, the transformation of the Asia-Pacific to the Indo-Pacific would have never happened.

Developments over the last quarter century have brought out that the India-ASEAN engagement has actually unleashed ideas, interests and forces that none of us could have foreseen at that time. At its most basic level, the relationship with ASEAN has contributed to changing Indian thinking, of society as much as policymakers. Exposures and interactions have through osmosis raised new expectations and ambitions. Some of these are today very apparent in Indian policy activities and debates.

Quite apart from encouraging economic reforms, ASEAN has influenced Indian thinking on a broader set of issues. For a start, it has facilitated the externalization of India to a great degree. Indeed, the new wave of Indian investment abroad began in South-East Asia. Singapore, of course, is a vivid example. The involvement with the ASEAN and the consequent trade and sourcing of resources has also significantly heightened maritime consciousness. This has led India not only to be more active in the pursuit of maritime interests but to conceptualize that domain for policy engagement. A focused and integrated Indian Ocean policy today is largely shaped by its experiences with ASEAN.

This interaction has also had a beneficial impact on India's own thinking about regionalism. It now seeks consciously to ensure that neighbours also benefit from its growth and prosperity. The growing number of regional infrastructure projects supported by India is a sign of its seriousness in this resolve.

ASEAN could also be credited with contributing significantly to India's understanding of the role that people of Indian origin abroad can play in its relationship with the world. Indeed, there are few better examples of networking and bridging than the diaspora of this region. Not least is the catalytic role that South-East Asia has played in the revival of India's historical linkages and interests. The Nalanda concept, as we know it today, literally started in Singapore. Since then, it has emerged as an encouragement to a broader Indian embrace of its Buddhist history and heritage and a more central place for that in its people-to-people contacts.

In the past, the contrasting world that existed east of India was a bridge too far for its strategic horizon. When the two worlds collided, as they did in the early 1960s, it was more to India's peril than benefit. But the engagement with ASEAN has begun a socialization process where India's interests eastwards have steadily developed. For this to gather momentum, both India and its eastern partners will have to step out of their comfort zone. Where such interests are supported by values, then convergences could take root more definitively. Whether the traditional outlook of nations can accommodate more contemporary concerns remains to be seen. India and Japan in particular have a gulf of mindsets to cross. Reconciling Indian improvization with Japanese perseverance requires a strong sense of purpose backed by sustained efforts. The test for this relationship is to overcome unfamiliarity and distance, very different from the usual problems of divergences and irritants. That politics is in command as Japan looks at India could well mean a lot. Because in reality, it is trade that follows the flag. If Noida and Nagoya are to truly meet, it would add a new page to Asia's history. And then there may yet be another twist in a continental saga that could be less predestined than many assume.

8

The Pacific Indian

A Re-emerging Maritime Outlook

———

*'You cannot cross the sea merely by standing and staring
at the water'*

— RABINDRANATH TAGORE

As the world changes, it will naturally throw up new concepts and terminology. 'Indo-Pacific' is among the more recent additions to the global strategic lexicon. Because Donald Trump used this term in the 2017 APEC Summit and the US Pacific Command was renamed as the Indo-Pacific one, Americans think that they invented it. The Japanese, however, believe the credit should really go to them. After all, Prime Minister Shinzo Abe spoke at the Indian Parliament of the 'Confluence of Two Oceans' more than a decade ago. Indians themselves are not to be left behind, underlining that the Indo-Pacific has been tossed around in their naval thinking even earlier. And by establishing a dedicated division in its Foreign Ministry, India has signalled its attachment even more strongly. Australians too rank among the list of claimants, and the ASEAN led by Indonesia has now tabled an Indo-Pacific outlook. Purists may actually award it to a German strategist of the 1930s, Karl Haushofer, even though his perspective was that of a Eurasian strategist. But, whatever its analytics, Indo-Pacific today owes its existence primarily to the compulsions of practitioners. The waters are changing as we speak and Indo-Pacific is not tomorrow's forecast but actually yesterday's reality.

Many things in the world come around. It is worth reflecting on the fact that the Royal Navy acted on an Indo-Pacific approach for decades without necessarily articulating the term. So today, as some powers aspire, others plan, a few prepare and the rest ponder, what drives the debate needs a clarity divorced from claims of ownership. Semantics should not obscure the fact that events are unfolding that give this concept a greater texture with each passing day. The Indo-Pacific naturally means different things to different powers, but it undeniably is a priority for all of them. For India, it is the logical next step beyond Act East and a transcending of the confines of South Asia. For Japan, the movement into the Indian Ocean could be part of its strategic evolution. For the US, a unified theatre addresses convergences that are central to its new posture. Russia, for its part, could visualize this as part of its new emphasis on the Far East. For Europe, it is a case for a return to a region from which it withdrew. And the stakes are particularly high for China, as its maritime capabilities are the prerequisite to its emergence as a global power.

This is unquestionably the arena for the contemporary version of the Great Game, where multiple players with diverse ambitions display their strategic skills. Their efforts at building convergences and understanding contestation will have a particular importance as it takes place on a global lifeline.

The Indo-Pacific may be in fashion as a strategic concept now. But it has been an economic and cultural fact for centuries. After all, Indians and Arabs have left their imprint all the way up to the eastern coast of China, just as the people of South-East Asia did on Africa. In fact, this reality is not remote at all and the seamlessness of waters only sharpened the appetite of the Western powers who entered it. The British Empire operated its own version of the Indo-Pacific that was neither free nor open. Its visualization of both resources and interests was across an integrated zone, explaining many of the events of the nineteenth and twentieth century.

Other powers, in turn, followed the approach of the dominant one. If Indian troops fought in the Boxer Rebellion, then the Japanese too came all the way to Singapore and Burma. And not least, it was the enormous logistical effort from India by the Anglo-American alliance that sustained China in its war against Japan after 1942. The earlier era of the Indo-Pacific lasted until 1945 and was reflected in the presence of British and American forces across the region. After the war, Indian troops were deployed in seven prefectures of Chugoku and Shikoku in Japan. And the 2/5 Gurkhas even mounted guard at the Imperial Palace in Tokyo. What separated the Indian and Pacific theatres thereafter was the global supersession of the UK by the US. That shifted the centre of gravity to the Pacific, strengthened thereafter by the revolution in China and the war in Korea. As for the UK, India's independence and its own falling back to the Gulf focused its interest westwards. The result was that a continuum gave way to narrower domains that were solidified by military command jurisdictions. The Indo-Pacific is as much our past as it is our future. Whether it is, therefore, strategically viable depends on the politics of the day, as it did before.

For our purposes, what is important is that just as the dominance of the US undid Indo-Pacific after 1945, American adjustments now can help reinvent it. This may happen not just by itself but because there are also other autonomous processes moving in the same direction. They include the ambitions of China, the interests of India, the posture of Japan, the confidence of Australia and the awareness of the ASEAN. Like alliances, strategic concepts also respond to times and the moment of Indo-Pacific has arrived again.

As with many other developments in the world today, the trigger for Indo-Pacific too is the change in the American stance and the rise of China. Because the former is more reactive, it makes sense to centre analysis around the latter. A decade ago, China debated vigorously and publicly the role of maritime power in its future. Part of that was to address a traditional strategic dilemma posed by the limitations of its eastern seaboard and multiple island chains beyond. But by 2009, there was also a larger quest which subsumed this argument. Chinese policymakers had already recognized that if that nation was to emerge as a global power, it must perforce be a maritime one. The ensuing debate upended a historical tradition quite comprehensively. In that sense, 2012 was not just a transition in political leadership but in strategic thinking as well.

The impact of global developments on the Indian Ocean could not have left India unaffected. Its location jutting into the centre gives that country a unique attribute. This strategic edge was, however, taken so much for granted that its maritime exploitation was always below par. As greater naval activity unfolded, India also had to contend with connectivity initiatives that had maritime implications. This now meant an oceanic focus for a power whose security horizons were already being stretched. The nature of the challenge is also novel since so much of it is played out in the global commons. The solution to this predicament inevitably was in the strengthening of capability, creation of balances and encouragement of cooperation. It is logical for India to work with those who value its influence, advocate a larger role for it and are comfortable with its activities.

As each major power has its own perspective, their narratives sometimes can be different. For India, it is all about the pathway of its own steady rise, while also responding to the compulsions arising from the posture of others. The East Asia Summit already took India beyond the Indian Ocean to the Indo-Pacific. Its participation in bilateral, trilateral and multilateral naval exercises in the Pacific Ocean carried its own significance. The steady externalization of its economy and focus towards the East made it sensitive to maritime security and safety. The conceptual justification for the Indo-Pacific, therefore, centres around the expanding interests of India. It is buttressed by its self-perception as a rule-abiding power that contributes to the global commons. Its core interests may be in the Indian Ocean, but a presence beyond also ensures a peaceful periphery. And since maritime activity has such a profound impact on overall equations, India's participation goes some way in contributing to stability in Asia.

While much of the attention focuses on the expansion of its interests, where India can really make a difference is in the Indian Ocean itself. This is not just a natural arena for its influence but one of overriding security consequence. By maintaining a strong posture there, India's value rises and ensures a more enthusiastic welcome further East. For India, getting its Indo-Pacific approach right rests on ensuring that it works out its Indian Ocean strategy even more correctly. After years of being in denial of a changing reality, India had to come to terms with the fact that there were now more forces at work in the oceans below. That acceptance drove the fashioning of the first integrated maritime outlook in 2015, appropriately articulated as SAGAR (Security and Growth for All in the Region). Premised on the belief that advancing cooperation and using our capabilities for larger good would benefit India, this has four key elements.

The first is to safeguard our mainland and islands, defend our interests, ensure a safe, secure and stable Indian Ocean, and make available our capabilities to others. The second focuses on deepening economic and security cooperation with our maritime neighbours and strengthening their capacities. The third envisages collective action and cooperation to advance peace and security and respond to emergencies. And the fourth seeks a more integrated and cooperative future for the region that enhances sustainable development. SAGAR drives a more active and outcome-oriented Indian approach that enhances its influence by delivering on partnerships. It is translated into hinterland linkages and strengthened regionalism, maritime contributions and support, and the creation of an extended neighbourhood. It comes with a willingness to assume responsibilities as a net security provider. Its impact is visible in more projects, initiatives and activities.

A comprehensive maritime strategy naturally has a set of priorities, best depicted in terms of concentric circles. The core is a maritime infrastructure for the homeland, development of island assets, connectivity to immediate neighbours, and the capabilities brought to bear on a daily basis. With regard to its Neighbourhood First policy, what is of particular relevance are those initiatives which have an oceanic impact. The next circle includes the maritime space beyond India's waters and its immediate island neighbours like Sri Lanka, Maldives, Mauritius and Seychelles. On land, the restoration of connectivity to the extended neighbourhood is high in importance. They have direct implications for the ability of India to safeguard waters on a larger scale.

Then comes the real challenge – the revival of the Indian Ocean as a community that builds on its historical and cultural foundations. It is only by shaping cooperation across the Indian Ocean that India can hope to significantly influence events beyond it. How to make the ocean a more seamless and cooperative space is not only a larger regional objective, but one that would enhance the centrality of India. These challenges, even if differing in nature and importance, need to be addressed in parallel as they are to be self-supporting. The outermost circle takes India into the Pacific, engaging convergent interests to ensure core security while also promoting a stable periphery. Developing the policy exchanges, capability exercises and cooperation mechanisms in that regard is work under progress. It is the interplay of these circles that will determine not only India's maritime future but its larger strategic posture as well.

The Act East policy and greater maritime activities are already leading to the revival of ports on India's eastern seaboard that were extinguished during the colonial period. But to take full advantage of its location, it is vital that connectivity to maritime facilities is expanded beyond India's borders. Bangladesh and Myanmar both hold considerable potential in this regard. The undertaking of connectivity and infrastructure projects by offering Lines of Credit is already ongoing. While the Kaladan project to Sittwe port and the Trilateral Highway to Thailand are among the bigger commitments to Myanmar, there is scope for expanding the linkages across the Bay of Bengal as well.

In its own territory too, there are plenty of other options that India can explore to strengthen its maritime influence. The development of the Andaman & Nicobar Islands would surely rank foremost. We should be asking ourselves how other nations would have utilized such a well-located asset. Whether it is Act East, SAGAR, Neighbourhood First or Indo-Pacific, strategy begins at home and it is really progress there that would be a test of seriousness.

In other circumstances, the re-energizing of SAARC should be one of India's key foreign policy priorities. South Asia is clearly among the least integrated regions of the world and being located at the centre of the Indian Ocean, its dysfunctionality affects that larger space directly. The case for building connectivity and expanding trade is glaringly obvious. However, determined opposition to the core agenda from one country undermines much needed cooperation. India, therefore, focuses more on aggregating bilateral and plurilateral initiatives for the moment. Eventually, the hope will be that normalcy will prevail in this area as in others. In the meanwhile, other options like BIMSTEC have to be developed, shifting the focus to the Bay of Bengal.

Strengthening the sense of extended neighbourhood is part of India's reclaiming of history. Its cultural basis is so visible that it needs little affirmation, whether in South-East Asia, the Gulf or Central Asia. Even its economic basis is now increasing gradually as trade, investment and mobility make their impact. What it really lacks is the connectivity underpinning that was disrupted seven decades ago. And the oceans can make a real difference in finding a fix.

The Indian Ocean has been described in one of its histories as a highway linking great multitudes across vast geographies. This critical role can actually be played once again if its centre of gravity acts as a facilitator. That requires a smoother movement of goods and people not only within India but also to its immediate neighbourhood, and beyond. Not coincidentally, stronger connectivity is at the heart of many of India's foreign policy initiatives. A growing commitment to trans-national highway construction, multi-modal transport initiatives, railway modernization, inland waterways, coastal shipping, and port development underlines its seriousness. In fact, better logistics has become the dominant theme of India's neighbourhood outreach.

India's experience westwards is less positive for reasons that the world knows well. Nevertheless, the Chabahar port project with Iran and the sea access it can provide for Afghanistan represent important openings. Iran's considerable potential as a transit corridor to Eurasia is worth exploring. So too is the larger International North-South Transport Corridor that can facilitate transportation to Russia and Europe, as well as the Ashgabat Agreement that connects the Indian Ocean to Central Asia. Developments in the Gulf and West Asia may provide still more options in the days ahead.

An Indian Ocean strategy naturally means paying more attention to its maritime neighbours. As is common in such cases, history and sociology are mixed blessings. Relationship-building is expressed in terms of political visibility, greater cooperation and more projects with Sri Lanka, Maldives, Mauritius and Seychelles. An integrated view is emerging of trade, tourism, infrastructure, environment, blue economy and security. India has also been partnering these countries in capability building by providing radars, coastal surveillance equipment, vessels and aircraft and by establishing maritime infrastructure. The cooperation agenda today covers white shipping, blue economy, disaster response, anti-piracy and counterterrorism, as well as hydrography. It was reassuring for these nations to see how staunchly India stood by them during the corona pandemic.

The importance of these maritime relationships to India's security interests cannot be overstated. After all, this is the core from which India could help build a larger pan-Indian Ocean architecture. It is therefore critical to ensure that this proximate zone remain sensitive to India's interests. It is also desirable that the Indian Ocean does not become an arena for intense competition. Island states will have their own sensitivities but also their calculations. While they may seek to make the best of their chances, the combination of political comfort, economic collaboration and cultural affinities will play its part. Responsibility for peace, prosperity, security and stability rests primarily on the approach of resident powers. Their collective thinking and cooperative action are the basis for greater community awareness. And the strongest arguments in favour lie in the ocean's history.

The Indian Ocean 'world' did once have an essential unity that was based on maritime trade rhythms. We also know that it was indeed a self-sustaining zone, albeit with natural and flexible boundaries, that set it apart from others proximate. The association of maritime trade with cultural influence was both graphic and pervasive across the ocean. As a result, traditions, practices, faiths and commerce created a virtual connectivity that overcame distance. The romance of history, however, had to give way to the realities of international relations as the arrival of the Europeans fragmented the ocean and its littoral. The postcolonial world also created new national, and thereafter, regional identities that put the ocean in the shade. Moreover, economic activity and cultural habits specific to the coast in the Indian Ocean did not always extend very far inland. This lack of depth perhaps also contributed to the strategic reduction of an entire eco-system into just a water space. The tension between socio-economics and geopolitics was largely responsible for this situation. Today, as the latter changes dramatically, the Indian Ocean cannot remain impervious.

As oceans go, the Indian Ocean is one that has been the beneficiary of a millennia of culture. While its fundamental economic activities directly derived from cycles of nature, these were also carried over into traditions. As a result, the ocean evolved its own special identity that is based on mobility, acceptance and inter-penetration. This historical inheritance is visible across its expanse, from Hindu temples in Bali and My Son, in fact all the way up to Zhengzhou on the Fujian coast of China; in Arab communities in Aceh and eastern Sri Lanka, or the Waqwaq settlers in Madagascar. Indeed, there are few more striking examples of global trends being expressed through the region as local presence. The remnants of influence after so many centuries only give us a partial sense of the intensity and vibrancy of what it must have been once. That they still tell their tale testifies to the fact that the overall ethos of the Indian Ocean was one of co-existence and adjustment, where respect for diversity was intrinsic to the promotion of trade. To revive a better sense of its own identity, it is important to appreciate and foster this multi-chromatic picture of the Indian Ocean.

Pluralism and syncretism are deep historical traits of the Ocean and they have been strengthened by liberalism as well. If we stop and think about it, the Indian Ocean is the most populous English-speaking lake in the world, larger than the Atlantic Ocean. The colonial era undoubtedly did much damage to this ocean community. But it also left behind institutions, practices and values that are naturally supportive of international norms and rule of law. A combination of history – both ancient and more recent – provide the foundation today to build a more contemporary region with its own personality.

But despite its legacy and its aspirations, the reality is that the unity of the Indian Ocean is not self-evident. The reasons for that are complex and worthy of a debate by themselves. In part, it was the effect of the lateral fragmentation of the region by external powers. Colonial domination created artificial firewalls through their administrative jurisdictions that diluted centuries of natural movements and contacts. Their salience also saw an accentuation in the divisions between the ocean and its littoral societies, with a shrinking of local maritime practices and capabilities.

As these inherent traditions of seafaring diminished due to European presence, we were left with a less active visualization of this vast global commons. The greatest disruption was the impact on the ocean culture by the fate of India. The reduction of its influence under colonial rule was aggravated by its partition. Both in reach and importance, the fulcrum of the ocean stood significantly diminished. Not just that, the emergence of modern nation states after decolonization again put such a strong emphasis on territoriality that it further reduced the salience of regional and trans-regional cooperation and flows. The Indian Ocean was thus seen as less intrinsically coherent than, say, the Atlantic or the Pacific. Even its smaller constituents, like the Bay of Bengal or the Arabian Sea, are not deemed to have a culture akin to the Mediterranean, the Caribbean or the North Sea. Rebuilding that will not be easy especially if there are powerful forces with contrary interests.

The Indian Ocean, like many other regions, must therefore find more solutions within. A key step in that direction is to create the connectivity that promotes a clearer personality to emerge. It is obviously unrealistic to just fall back on the past monsoon-driven one, though we should not underestimate the attractions of soft connectivity. The problem is that littoral nations, in the last five decades, have each joined a regional grouping, some of them more than one. Going across the ocean, we have a parade of acronyms that testify to its fractures: SADC, GCC, SAARC, BIMSTEC, ASEAN, EAS, etc. Encouraging nations and regions to work towards a composite Indian Ocean one is, therefore, not easy. None probably would be opposed, but few actually have the necessary enthusiasm.

At a diplomatic level, promoting greater interaction among these groupings would itself make a contribution. It is also useful to bridge physically the boundaries between them. A good example is the India-Myanmar border where SAARC meets ASEAN. While land connectivity is obviously critical, we must also recognize that the underdevelopment of maritime infrastructure is itself largely responsible for the profile of the Indian Ocean. No less significant is hinterland development. Part of the Indian Ocean's limitation was the narrowness of its coastal culture. As unified national societies emerged in Asia, the psychological distance from the ocean also narrowed. Hinterland economies have increasingly become linked to maritime trade. It is apparent today that the development of their infrastructure can be a game changer in elevating the importance of the Indian Ocean.

The centrality of the Indian Ocean to global trade and development is not a fresh realization. After all, it covers one-fifth of the world's total ocean area and encapsulates coastlines of almost 70,000 km. But more than the expanse, it is about location. With Asia's economic revival, whether we see the region as markets or production centres, transportation of goods has only acquired greater salience. The flow of natural resources is correspondingly growing with this ocean now accounting for two-thirds of the world's maritime oil trade. More than two-fifths of the world's population lives around the ocean. Ensuring the smooth and uninterrupted flow of one-third of the world's bulk cargo and half its container traffic is not a small responsibility. With the passage of time, it must also become an increasingly collective one.

India takes this challenge seriously and is prepared to shoulder its responsibilities fully. We have started to conclude white shipping agreements and cooperate on coastal and EEZ surveillance with some of our immediate neighbours. India participates in arrangements like the ReCAAP and the SOMS 10 mechanism for maritime safety. We have also taken an active role in fighting piracy, both to our West and East. Since 2008, we have continued to conduct anti-piracy patrols in the Gulf of Aden and other maritime routes in the region. The Indian Navy has undertaken about fifty anti-piracy escort missions. It has contributed overall to greater maritime safety in the region and enabled the reduction of the High-Risk Area in December 2015, thereby cutting shipping insurance costs.

Security challenges in the Indian Ocean are addressed by each player in their own way. In India's case, they are essentially an outcome of national capabilities, buttressed by participation in relevant regional bodies. The ASEAN Regional Forum, in particular, is evaluated highly by India as a broad-based platform. Closer to home, India is developing trilateral cooperation with Sri Lanka and Maldives. Where naval interests are concerned, the steady growth of the thirty-five-nation Indian Ocean Naval Symposium (IONS) over the last decade has been a very encouraging development. It has helped to promote a shared understanding of maritime issues, enhance regional maritime security, strengthen capabilities, establish cooperative mechanisms, develop inter-operability and provide speedy responses.

Moving from policy to performance, it is evident that navies working together in pursuit of shared security goals have a stabilizing impact. India participates in a number of bilateral exercises with Singapore, Sri Lanka, France and Australia, amongst others. In addition, we partner the US and Japan for the Malabar set of exercises. To some of the Indian Ocean island states, India has supplied naval equipment, provided training and undertaken hydrographic services. And its maritime horizons today clearly include partners in East Africa.

Reconstituting a community identity in the Indian Ocean is a painstaking endeavour. In its structured format, it would require oceanic forums like the Indian Ocean Rim Association (IORA) to acquire greater content and higher profile. But that perhaps is an overly formal way of approaching what is a complex challenge. Getting a large number of countries with distinctive histories and diverse cultures to collect around a shared ocean space requires both institutional and informal solutions. Building blocks do exist, once we start thinking of them in that manner.

In this uncertain world, if there is a point of agreement, it is that the salience of alliances is decreasing. It is equally apparent that old-fashioned military rivalries are giving way to more subtle competitions for influence. The future is to get nations whose interests are aligned or even overlap to work together. That would mean agendas and conversations with a more open mind. And an appreciation for what each player can bring to the table. This trend is visible already in naval exercises, strategic consultations or infrastructure projects.

Stability and order cannot be built only on the strength of capabilities. It must be tempered by the discipline of law, in this case respect for UNCLOS, which was recognized by IORA as the constitution for the oceans. Recognizing the growing importance of maritime trade in an increasingly globalized world, India supports freedom of navigation and overflight, and unimpeded commerce, based on the principles of international law, as reflected notably in the UNCLOS. India also believes that States should resolve disputes through peaceful means without threat or use of force and exercise self-restraint in the conduct of activities that could complicate or escalate disputes affecting peace and stability. Sea lanes of communication are critical for peace, stability, prosperity and development. As a State Party to the UNCLOS, India has urged all parties to show utmost respect for the convention, which establishes the international legal order of the seas and oceans. It is also our position that the authority of Annex VII Tribunal and its awards is recognized in Part XV of the UNCLOS itself.

If the Indian Ocean is now to occupy a more prominent place in the global political discourse, its best hope is the further development of the IORA. Over two decades, this body has harmonized multiple diversities to create a mixed ethos. It creates common ground for regional economic cooperation and provides opportunities to develop shared interests. It also encourages close interaction of business, academic institutions, scholars and the peoples of the member states. India is committed to building up the rim association in line with its own expanding bilateral ties in the region. It sees merit in the expansion and further invigoration of its activities, from renewable energy and the blue economy to maritime safety and security, water science and greater institutional and think-tank networking.

Given the history and traditions of the Indian Ocean, it is but appropriate that any serious effort at promoting its coherence would address issues of its unity and identity. We must take full advantage of the ties of kinship and family that span the Indian Ocean and are an important part of its history. But more active initiatives are also needed and Project Mausam, whose very nomenclature, which is based on the distinctive wind system of the Indian Ocean, signifies interest in the characteristics of the region.

The project promotes archaeological and historical research on cultural, commercial and religious interactions. It has become a vehicle for knowledge exchanges, networking and publications. If this is an example of a contemporary initiative to revive the Ocean's identity, there are many other supporting endeavours that contribute to the same objective. By raising interest in traditional knowledge and practices such as ayurveda and yoga, by rekindling interest in the journey of faiths like Buddhism or Sufism, or by utilizing powerful symbols like Nalanda or Ramayana to promote human exchanges, we are step by step adding to the consciousness of an eco-system that was once secure in its vibrancy.

Clearly, much depends on how the possibilities of connectivity unfold in Asia. There are today various approaches and initiatives that offer choices to the nations of this region. Many would understandably like to make the best of all these opportunities. But the experiences of the last decade underline the importance of making mature and considered decisions in this regard. If connectivity is not to acquire sharp strategic meaning, then there must be credible assurances that projects are not used to exert influence. Similarly, unviable projects open up the possibility of being leveraged. It is also vital that sovereignty is respected, and disputed areas avoided in such endeavours. Connectivity must widen flows, not direct them.

The ethos of the Indian Ocean is a consultative one and in the long run, it is the people-centric initiatives and projects that are likely to be more sustainable. While we tend to think of connectivity in physical terms, let us not forget that it has its softer aspects that are actually no less important. People-to-people contacts, religious travel and exchanges, heritage conservation and cultural promotion are all enabling factors that can contribute to a greater sense of bonding among societies. It is, therefore, essential that we approach the connectivity challenge with a holistic perspective – community-centred, not transactional – that has a purpose of common good as its primary driving force.

No analysis of the Indian Ocean would be complete without capturing the development at its extremities, be they the eastern coast of Africa or the Pacific Islands. The holding of Pacific Islands Summits and the enhancement of our engagements and development projects is important to the realization of our shared goal of climate justice. The story of India in Africa has similarly not got the attention it deserves, partly because it does not play to the gallery. Ties with East African countries on the Indian Ocean periphery with whom we have longer historical contact and closer proximity are particularly relevant to the Indo-Pacific debate.

The Indian Ocean is about people, culture and commerce. Appreciating its complex texture and intricate nuances is essential to nurture its growth and resurgence. It should be approached with empathy, not as a business. It must be treated as a partner, not as an arena. The goal must be interdependence, not dominance. While the monsoons may no longer dictate when ships can travel, yet its rhythms still pervade the lives of billions of people. The Ocean is renewing its status as a zone of encounters and crossroads of culture. The time is approaching for it to come back into its own, which is critical to the prospects of the Indo-Pacific.

To realize that India must take a contributing approach that partners others to build their capacity and secure interests. At another, it must be consultative in this engagement, whether bilateral or regional, or even in respect to the maritime commons. The willingness to shoulder greater responsibility must continue. After all, it is in one sense a maritime variant of our proud tradition of UN peacekeeping. Equally important is the message of respect for international law and norms, where India's behaviour speaks louder than any words. Responding to extra-regional powers and establishing new equations with intra-regional ones will shape an emerging architecture. The focus must be on getting understandings in place with multiple partners, so that a more diverse balance emerges. It is especially important to reassure ASEAN about its place in the Indo-Pacific, as that grouping has driven all serious regional discussions in the past. Both literally and conceptually, this is an opportunity to enhance its centrality.

If there is a definitive articulation of India's Indo-Pacific approach, that could be in Prime Minister Modi's address to the Shangri-La Dialogue in Singapore in 2018. Its vision was of a free, open and inclusive region that had South-East Asia – which connected the two oceans – at its centre. This was underpinned by a belief in a common rules-based order that applied to all states individually as well as to the global commons. This meant that all nations have equal access as a right under international law to the use of common spaces on sea and in air. Freedom of navigation, unimpeded commerce and peaceful settlement of disputes are also to be guaranteed. The economic component of the vision was of a level-playing field for all while connectivity underlined the importance of trust and respect for sovereignty, transparency, viability and sustainability. In essence, this was a call for an Asia of cooperation, rather than of rivalry.

The future of the Indo-Pacific lies in a complex range of forces interacting on a continuous basis. As with so many other facets of international relations today, this too has many open questions. For India, it will be an important element of its relationship with China and its partnership with the West. New possibilities could be opened up with Russia, whose maritime interests may grow with the viability of Arctic commerce. The importance of the Indo-Pacific to ties with Japan, ASEAN and Australia clearly cannot be underestimated.

The sea may have determined global politics two centuries ago and then receded in its salience. Perhaps we overstated its diminution as a factor in transforming world affairs, especially when a global power arrives on the stage. There are strategies at work, some obvious and others less so. The point of agreement is the criticality of a theatre that is re-emerging through the fusion of its predecessors. It is natural that a new discourse accompanies the changes in global order. Western terminology has long been on the table. China has advocated a new type of great power relations, a Belt and Road Initiative as well as a 'community of shared future of humankind'. India's world view is consultative, democratic and equitable, but must find clearer expression. When it comes to the Indo-Pacific, we will absorb changes in terminology, just as we come to terms with power shifts and their implications.

After the Virus

An Epilogue

'The world is a great gymnasium where we come to make
ourselves strong'

— SWAMI VIVEKANANDA

E ven otherwise, our world was moving discernibly towards an era of greater disruption, stronger nationalism, sharper competitiveness and a questioning of rules and regimes. And along came a virus that first devastated Wuhan and then proceeded to engulf the entire world. Quite apart from the enormous number of deaths it caused, millions have lost their livelihood across nations. Societies that were confident of their future saw the prospect of growth evaporate before their very eyes. Many, not just in India, who would have otherwise come out of poverty will have to wait longer. And all this because of a pandemic of which they had little knowledge and even less control. Considering its enormous impact, it cannot be that this extraordinary happening will be absorbed so easily by the world. Debates around it have broken out, sharpening arguments that were already in play. As a result, the pace of what was already underway will surely accelerate. Global contradictions will accentuate as geopolitics and geo-economics get more heated. Many characteristics of our turbulent era will get validated, perhaps even enhanced. And new wrinkles will be added to a more complicated world.

Partly because of how the pandemic unfolded, it has fed strongly into a US-China dynamic that is in flux. As it is, this particular relationship was busy grappling with issues of ambitions, intentions and interests. An American view of economic security being central to national security had put pressure on offshoring practices and global supply chains, while also enhancing technology sensitivity. But after the coronavirus, there is now an additional layer of health security being added to the mix. The availability of medicines, masks, personal protective equipment and testing kits during the pandemic graphically brought out national vulnerabilities across the world. How much post-pandemic sentiment would affect business judgements, especially on global supply chains, is therefore a natural concern. A shift in American thinking that goes beyond the Administration of the day now believes that a single-minded pursuit of efficiency and profits at the cost of the social fabric and industrial capabilities is unacceptable. Particularly in a climate of disrupted travel and health uncertainty, the risks of doing business abroad have increased. If, at the same time, policy uncertainty is also heightened, there will be much more pressure on the world that we know.

Even accepting that businesses are more deeply rooted than policy debates often suggest, it is hard to deny that the post-corona world will be very different. Comparatively at least, we will see more de-globalization, regionalization, de-coupling, self-reliance and shorter supply chains. As conversations about them get more animated, there is less pretence that we are also talking about the parallel world of political influence. Trade has never been without its politics and technology had provided a further overlay. The pandemic has now given this a more distinct edge. The relative merits of costs, risk and resilience in a globalized economy has become a more energized debate. It not only focuses on geographical dependence but sectoral ones as well. As a result, a greater awareness of strategic autonomy in the economic sphere has started to develop. In parallel, the concept of trusted partners has moved beyond the technology domain to a larger definition. As the ambit of what is perceived as security and sufficiency broadens, so too will the political connotations that surround it. Arguments about the nature of governance have also come more alive in this context. The prospect of parallel universes in different domains may have become stronger as a result. Whether it would all actually lead to a serious degree of 'decoupling' is the great imponderable. Trade dependency in itself is also becoming a more sensitive matter. Over the last decade, we have seen it used as a pressure point on occasions. As this recurs more often, it will induce a greater caution about the strategic nature of trade engagement.

The irony of the entrenched power being revolutionary and the rising one defending selective elements of the status quo has already been noted. As pressures increase, the contestation could become serious and create new narratives. Already, there has been a shift from marketing peaceful rise to declaring the arrival of wolf warriors. We may see much more of this on all sides. In many ways, the role reversal in world affairs will be even more stunning after the virus. The sense of victimhood is also visibly shifting location. Concerns about dependency and insecurity about dominance is similarly changing.

If the virus has aggravated differences and further politicized the economy, its impact on self-interest is no less. Corona nationalism is now its latest incarnation. During the pandemic, we have seen nations pursue their health security goals with little regard for the welfare of others. Some used their economic clout openly, while others forgot their regional solidarity. The few exceptions that did happen really did not compensate for this broad behavioural pattern. Now, much of that could be attributed to the panic generated by the virus. But what it did bring out was how international relations is practised in reality. If collective endeavours fray so quickly under stress, their future is clearly less than assured in an era of sustained pressure.

This then brings us to the state of multilateralism. That it could not rise effectively to the occasion has hardly enhanced its stature. Quite apart from controversies in that domain, there was little visible leadership when it came to defining the agenda or setting directions. What it reminds us is that the quality of multilateralism is eventually dependent on the extent of consensus among major powers. And that, as we all know, has been in short supply for some time. As a result, bodies and agendas have themselves become a trial of strength rather than a common landing zone. Striking a balance between national interest and global good has become harder as conversations focus more on influencing institutions. As a consequence, plurilateralism will be the beneficiary because it has a purpose and commonality now found wanting in multilateralism. The pursuit of resilient supply chains, especially in the health domain, could well be added to its growing agenda.

Leave alone multilateralism, even our understanding of globalization has changed as a result of recent developments. Till now, the common approach was to view it as a balance of multiple national interests, rather than an outcome of collective choice. Its economic perspectives were dominant, with primacy given to trade and investment. But as with the case of climate change or terrorism, pandemics have now demonstrated that there are issues on which no one can really stay out. Such realities cannot be a subject of calculations or negotiations as they reflect a more indivisible existence. If the world were to draw the right lessons, then this experience has the potential to reframe the debate on global issues. But for that to happen, it is imperative to find more common ground on the very questions that are today sources of contention.

Perhaps the most unpredictable impact of the pandemic is on the political fortunes of those in the societies most severely affected. It goes without saying that regimes in office would be judged by the quality of their response. And that, in turn, could be influenced by the narratives they create. What we do know is that the economic devastation resulting from the coronavirus has fundamentally changed the political calculations that preceded it. But they should still be factored in, as some of the thought processes could outlive those who introduced it into the contemporary discourse. The expectation that we may easily return to the past was never really well-founded. The coronavirus has probably made it even more difficult.

So where does all of this leave India? It is a polity which would strengthen stability and add to reassurance at a time of global volatility. Its influence will contribute to world rebalancing and shape the pace of multipolarity, political or economic. Its strong bonding with the global South is critical to ensuring that developmental priorities and natural justice are not disregarded. As an advocate of reformed multilateralism, it can support genuine collective endeavours even in a more nationalistic era. And as a civilizational power coming back on the global stage, it would be another powerful example of return of history.

Today's India also demonstrates that the spread of democracy can lead to a more vivid expression of beliefs and traditions. When combined with a strong determination to address neglected challenges of governance, this would inevitably generate new conversations. At the same time, India's progress in social development has the potential to make it a key source of trusted talent for the global knowledge-based economy. These are some of the factors as the world examines the accommodation that will inevitably accompany India's rise. How they deal with each other will reflect a mix of compulsions and convergences, whether they be of geopolitics, technology, markets or culture.

Naturally, India too will be shaped by the broad trends in the global environment that the coronavirus will intensify. But more than that, it needs to take into account the more direct consequences of the pandemic. Its destructive impact naturally demands a strategy of national revival. And that, in turn, warrants a fundamental rethink about our growth model. This was probably coming anyway, given how much the current economic framework has hollowed out our manufacturing capacities. In the context of the free trade agreements, there was already an ongoing debate about the adequacy of our preparations to engage the global economy more intensively. What was evident was that many concerns stemming from the policies of our partners remain unaddressed. Competing against those with structural advantages has been difficult, as evidenced by the growing trade deficit. Going further down that very pathway without a course correction has obvious implications. There are direct livelihood and social stability consequences. It is paradoxical that those urging India to be more open are themselves very sensitive on this score. A revival strategy, therefore, needs to be chalked out with the utmost deliberation. Whatever the choices we make on compatibility or engagement, there are some facts we simply cannot ignore.

As India has discovered in the past, economic strategies have to be in consonance not only with its own national situation, but the global one as well. If we are significantly out of step with the world, as we were by 1991, then they are difficult to sustain. Three decades later, India's capabilities, competitiveness and trade are under stress, this time for very different reasons. The post-1991 belief that we could rely on the costing of others abroad to build our own businesses at home clearly has a high price. A lowest bidder syndrome and obsessive quest for profit margins has ended up eroding domestic capabilities. Even more, the efficiency of others, instead of spurring competitiveness, has actually led to putting off further reforms. Openness abroad ironically has led to stagnation at home, discouraging innovation and killing creativity. MSMEs have borne the brunt of the damage. While the pandemic may have brought out weaknesses pertaining to health security, it has also exposed this larger strategic complacency. Other domains struggle similarly with their own predicaments. Whether it is unfair advantages that competitors enjoy or the lack of a level playing field, we need to predicate policy on realities rather than rhetoric. And the access we give and the arrangements we enter into must take those into account.

If we are to take stock, it could begin with the realization that the world has been more protectionist and one-sided than we expected. Our trade figures tell their own tale. Continuing to follow the post-1991 mantras in such circumstances makes little sense. Both national circumstances and global situation call for a much greater emphasis on self-reliance (Atmanirbharta). Such a policy outlook would encourage approaches that would be more self-generating and self-sustaining. By its very performance, there would be greater innovation and creativity. It is only when its own production flourishes at home that India can make an economic difference abroad. Therefore, a greater emphasis on Make in India, obviously not just for India but for the world.

We must also be more caring of our own interests and support them to compete globally. And certainly, our home turf should not be left wide open to those who close their own so firmly. Where India is a late-starter, what it takes to catch up must always be factored into policies. And these must aggressively promote employment, skills, innovation and commercialization. As many other polities do, there must be no hesitation in standing up for sensitive sectors. The narrow economic interests that drove past policies cannot prevail over the welfare of the many. This is not to make a case for autarchy but to argue for a greater capacity-building so central to comprehensive national power. Current times clearly mandate that every nation must have cards to play in the global arena; big nations especially so.

As the world moves towards greater diversification, the case for enhanced participation in global value chains will strengthen further. India can move more purposefully in this direction, but it must balance that with building up its domestic capabilities. A more capable India that will emerge as a result of greater self-reliance will surely also have more to offer. Far from turning its back on the world, India is actually preparing to participate more but with better preparation. After all, Atmanirbhar Bharat does coexist with Vasudhaiva Kutumbakam (the world is a family).

Rising in the midst of global turbulence, a lot will depend on India's ability to distinguish itself from others. The post-corona world is likely to see an even greater deficit in global goods. The demand for early responders and generous partners is therefore likely to be more. This was visible during the pandemic and Indian behaviour holds some clues to how it could develop further. By going the extra mile to provide medicines to more than 120 nations, two-thirds of them as grant, a clear message of internationalism was sent. Four medical missions were mounted in the same period to the Maldives, Kuwait, Mauritius and Comoros. In doing so, India not only established its credentials as the pharmacy of the world but also as a health security responder. Equally, what is evident is that greater Indian capacities will make themselves felt on world affairs as part of a conscious strategy.

The last few years have demonstrated a growing Indian capacity to contribute to the global discourse and make a difference to international outcomes. We have significantly shaped the connectivity debate and backed that up with a plethora of projects, including in our immediate neighbourhood. Our single-minded campaign against terrorism has brought that issue into sharp focus in key world forums. Where maritime security and HADR situations are concerned, India has emerged as a key player, especially in the Indian Ocean.

At the political level, our confidence in overcoming the hesitations of history has opened up new space. Strategic clarity has helped to exploit that more effectively. Overall, the Indian persona is much more in evidence in a variety of ways. Our footprint has visibly grown in Africa, as also in many other regions where past connections were weaker. Indeed, this combination of significant engagement and deeper collaboration that extends across continents prepares us for a global mindset. The world may be on the threshold of a new decade; but India is ready for the next phase of its own evolution.

The world we are poised to enter is a subject of intense argumentation. It is further complicated by transformational changes in politics, economics and technology. Coming to terms with the declining shelf-life of the old post-1945 order is itself difficult. It is a still bigger challenge to fully recognize the elements which drive the one in the making. Assumptions of various dimensions are being questioned, at home as well as abroad. What we can just about agree upon is that the world is in the midst of a real transition. And our reading of the directions we head is influenced by our own preferences, interests, viewpoints and hopes.

The India Way, especially now, would be more of a shaper or decider rather than just be an abstainer. This has been already visible on debates like climate change and connectivity. India must be a just and fair power as well, consolidating its position as a standard bearer of the global South. At home, it would not only address its developmental challenges more effectively but also acquire faster the characteristics of a modern society and nation state. And finally, the India Way would express its brand with growing confidence, whether in its civilizational attributes or in its contemporary achievements.

For an approach of self-reliance to succeed, it must be accompanied by a greater sense of self-confidence. In India's case, the decisiveness with which it has addressed varied challenges in the last few years provides enough grounds for that. This mindset will be even more needed in the post-corona world of individualistic behaviour. Some of that would be expressed in an ability to set our own priorities and define our own solutions. But there will also be the pressures of a competitive world that go beyond convergence and transactions. Making its choices to advance its interests should come naturally to a polity so deeply steeped in an independent ethos. In the past, that may have made us an outlier. Today, it could well be the norm.

As we are regarded with greater interest by other societies, a natural consequence is to probe India's likely approach to key contemporary issues. Our answers – indeed our conduct – in that regard will also define what is the India Way. Comparisons will inevitably be made as others try to fit us into a model. But as with our use of capabilities, the choices that we make would also have few precedents. In putting out our narrative, ethics, culture and history may constitute part of the answer. But there are more domains as well that are relevant. India cannot escape the ideological battles of the day, however complex they may be. Challenging orthodox beliefs and viewpoints will always be controversial. Especially, if a sense of morality is attributed to the past and change is made to look risky. Some of the sharper lines drawn recently may, however, get blurred as the post-corona world throws up new challenges. But on its part, a more confident

India should take these debates in its stride as part and parcel of a larger global rebalancing.

The rise of India, like other aspects of international relations, is a story without an ending. It may not always unfold smoothly, sometimes for reasons that are beyond our control. But, each generation passes on the torch to the next, hopefully a little brighter. In that process we have to constantly remedy the past while preparing for the future. Sound policymaking, even in the best of times, is therefore an exercise of both review and planning. The corona experience, however, gives that an exceptional value as we prepare for a challenge that is truly without precedent. None of us could have foreseen the enormity of what has just happened or indeed its implications that are still unfolding. Who will be hit to what extent by the pandemic, and who will recover and reinvent are still question marks. But, despite such an extraordinary degree of uncertainty, India must stay with a game plan that remains valid even now. Its elements may be more complicated and its challenges more daunting. But a stronger competitive spirit and a sharper strategic sense will surely stand us in good stead.

The world is clearly not what it was until just recently. In its systemic impact, the coronavirus may be the most consequential global happening after 1945. In an immediate sense, it would add to global turbulence by encouraging policy departures across geographies. The paradox the world will confront is to seek change in the very order in which it is still deeply invested. Some have already mastered that art well, while others still struggle. A more fragmented, diffused and complicated future awaits, as all of us will now do our political sums differently.

The value of India in such global calculations is apparent. It will probably increase even further after the virus. So, let take it as a sign of the times that the world has discovered the virtue of Namaste, the India Way of greeting with folded hands.

Index

INDEX

About the Author

Dr S. Jaishankar is currently the External Affairs Minister of India and was appointed to that position in May 2019. He is a Member of Parliament in the Rajya Sabha (Upper House) representing the state of Gujarat.

His career as a professional diplomat for more than four decades culminated with a three-year tenure as the Foreign Secretary from 2015 to 2018. During that period, he was also a member of the Atomic Energy Commission and the Space Commission.

Before that, he served as the Ambassador of India to the United States of America during the Obama Administration from 2013 to 2015. He moved there from China, where he was the longest serving Indian Ambassador, from 2009 to 2013. His other ambassadorial positions are those to Singapore from 2007 to 2009 and to the Czech Republic from 2000 to 2004.

Earlier diplomatic assignments included those in Moscow, Washington DC and Colombo as a Political Officer, Budapest as a Commercial Counsellor and Tokyo as the Deputy Chief of Mission. In the Ministry of External Affairs, he was the Head of the Americas Division from 2004 to 2007 and Director of the East Europe Division from 1993 to 1994. He also served as the Press Secretary to the President of India from 1994 to 1996.

After his diplomatic career, he was President (Global Corporate Affairs) at Tata Sons Private Limited during 2018-19.

Dr S. Jaishankar is a graduate of St Stephen's College at the University of Delhi. He has an MA in Political Science and an MPhil and PhD in International Relations on nuclear diplomacy from Jawaharlal Nehru University, Delhi.

He was a recipient of the Padma Shri award in 2019.